How to Write Rules That People Want to Follow

3rd Edition

A Guide to Writing

Respectful Policies and Directives

Lewis S. Eisen

pixley press

COPYRIGHT INFORMATION

CATALOGING IN PUBLICATION DATA

Eisen, Lewis S., 1957-
    How to Write Rules that People Want to Follow, 3rd Edition

978-1-988749-06-8 Paperback
978-1-988749-07-5 ePub
978-1-988749-08-2 .mobi
978-1-988749-09-9 .pdf

1. Business and Economics — Business Communications/General.
2. Business and Economics — Business Writing. 3. Business and Economics — Leadership. 4. Law — Legal Writing.

DEDICATION

To John Byers, a police officer who taught me that even in one-sided control situations, the dominant power can still give orders respectfully.

"Do thou restrain the haughty spirit in thy breast, for better far is gentle courtesy."

~ Homer (800 BC - 700 BC)

CONTENTS

FOREWARD

by Carol Ring, FCPA   CEO, Culture Connection
www.carolring.ca

Recognized as one of Canada's
    Top 100 Most Powerful Women

For more than 35 years I've been passionate about building high performing teams. I see these teams as a way not only for our businesses to succeed, but also as a path to releasing the full potential of each person in our organization.

As a specialist in company culture transformation, I am always on the look out for experts whose work can support and compliment the creation of workplaces that allow people to do their very best work. And that's how Lewis Eisen came into my life.

We met over coffee at a local Starbucks. I was curious about Lewis's work in the written rule world. Many people believe that culture is all about the behaviours of the leaders and how that sets the tone for the organization. However, tone can also be set by our physical surroundings at work, our reward and recognition programs, and most definitely by internal written communications.

I remember being in Sudbury for a keynote speech presentation. I arrived the night before, checked in at the front desk of my hotel and quickly dropped off my luggage in the room. I was starving, and was looking forward to heading across the street for a bite to eat and a glass of wine.

As I trotted down the stairs, I came across an interesting sign:

> # DO NOT LEAVE ANYTHING IN THIS HALL EVER! INCLUDING GARBAGE –
>
> # IT IS AN EMERGENCY EXIT ONLY!

Yes, it was written in all caps.

This "rule" made me wonder if it was for staff or for hotel guests? What were people leaving in the stairwell that would cause such a reaction? What type of hotel was I in?

I instantly thought of Lewis and how this business could really use his help.

How to Write Rules That People Want to Follow is not merely a technical guide of how to structure your policies, procedures, or guidelines. It's much deeper than that. In this book you'll learn to dig into the real purpose of the rule you're trying to create and how best to achieve that outcome. After all, there's no point in writing a rule if no one follows it.

The command-and-control management style has almost completely disappeared. It's no longer an effective way to lead. But has your written communication evolved as well? As Lewis says, "rules that sound like they were written by angry parents scolding naughty children are no longer appropriate."

I love that phrase! It's no badge of honour to have a thick book of policies. One of my previous employers had a policy manual that was 3 binders! No wonder we didn't know what we were supposed to do. Who had time to read and internalize all this information?

I regularly recommend this book to my clients as part of our work to align the many aspects of their organizations. It is only with alignment that a culture can become great. Your purpose, strategy, brand promise, and culture must all be congruent. And so must your rules.

This book is about writing better rules. But it's really about creating better workplaces so people can do their very best work. Get ready to make a difference to the people in your organization!

September, 2020

PREFACE TO THE 3RD EDITION

Initially, I didn't realize that the notion of "revising policies to sound respectful" would resonate with so many people.

Since the first edition of this book, published in 2017, I have seen the idea spread. The more courteous approach to rule writing has been adopted by policy writing groups at a wide variety of organizations — business, government, and not-for-profit associations — spanning the U.S., Canada, the U.K., and Australia.

In 2019 the book became an Amazon international best-seller in a number of categories, including Business Writing, Business Communication, Business Reference, and Human Resources and Personnel Management.

One of the drivers to produce a new edition was my wish to look at codes of conduct. Having come across several harshly worded versions ordering me to be a nice person, I realized that this type of document was even more misunderstood than typical policy documents. You'll find a new chapter on codes of conduct, along with some notes about ethical codes.

You'll also find a new chapter devoted entirely to a discussion of "must," "may," and "should." Not only have those terms become antiquated — being based on an underlying assumption of a Parent–Child dynamic — they are also ambiguous in far too many contexts. The availability of wording that's both clearer and less condescending permits us to challenge the traditional view that those modal verbs are fundamental to policy writing.

You'll note that I collect real-life samples for illustrative purposes. I'm always on the lookout for poorly drafted policy documents and rudely worded signs; they make great examples for teaching purposes. If you come across something that's particularly egregious, feel free to send it to me at <leisen@pfx.ca>.

Successes make great stories, too, and I love hearing about them. If what you read in this book leads you to revise any of your current policy documents, feel free to send me "before" and "after" copies.

As with all my previous publications, I rely on other people to let me know when my writing is unclear. Thanks to Fern Lebo, author of many books on an impressive variety of topics, whose feedback and insights on the first two editions were invaluable. Thanks also to Jeff Whited, Brenda Platt, Shari at PrestigeProofreading.ca, and Joyce Eisen who proofread this third edition. Their sharp eyes have helped me feel confident that words are properly used, that I have not dangled any participles unnecessarily, and that punctuation, typography, and style choices are consistent throughout the text. Their recommendations helped bring the writing to its present form.

INTRODUCTION

When I was a little boy, every night I would sit with my family around the dinner table. My parents had a consistent rule: if you didn't eat the main course — including the vegetables — then you didn't get dessert. You may have grown up with a similar rule.

Our parents and teachers have given us so many rules over the years that we barely even notice them when we move into the business world.

People in organizations make a lot of rules. They make rules for their employees, for their customers, and for their visitors. They might call these rules "policies," or "standards," or "terms and conditions," but basically they are rules for others to follow. Rules are ubiquitous.

While some people resent the imposition of rules in some cases, rules are and will continue to be a fact of life. We need them to maintain a civil society. Without rules, we would be constantly bumping into one another, both literally — on the highways — and figuratively — when we all try to speak at once in a meeting.

Barking Orders

The problem is that **too many organizational rules sound aggressive and confrontational**. Look at the examples in panel 1.

Panel 1

Visitors are **prohibited** from entering the service area.

Returns are **strictly forbidden**. Customers must check all merchandise carefully before leaving the store.

Loud conversation is **not tolerated**.

Can you hear the tone of voice in these statements? They sound more like military orders than rules. The tone of voice is not just assertive; it's downright bossy.

If that tone of voice doesn't bother you, it's only because you're used to hearing it. So many people spout off rules that sound like imperial commands that we often don't give the tone of voice a second thought.

But why? Why the need to put anyone on the defensive? After all, these rules are written for adults, not children. Why doesn't the wording of the rule take that into account? We're at the workplace, not the playground. Why do the rules sound like angry parents or teachers scolding naughty children?

Sadly, the most common answer is "because it's always been done that way." This answer is offered by all types of organizations, both for-profit and not-for-profit, public and private, large and small.

The truth is that policies and rules don't have to talk down to us. With the proper wording, they can actually sound like one adult respectfully and courteously talking to another.

The Origin of That Wording

How did this happen? How did we end up with so many harsh-sounding rules?

It's actually not hard to figure out. We grew up learning rule-making from our parents, teachers, and other caregivers. That's the way they spoke to us.

Unfortunately, as we were growing up what we learned about rule-making was that rules should sound dictatorial. Presumably, this approach was meant to reinforce the fact that the rule makers were completely in charge and were serious about what they were requiring.

The rules were typically expressed in a standard formula:

If you do x, then expect y

where x represents a wrong action and y represents the threatened punishment.

My parents' dinnertime dessert rule uses that formula: if you don't eat your vegetables, then you don't get dessert. A bad action leads to a bad consequence. Avoid the bad action, and you avoid the bad consequence.

Re-evaluating That Formula

We may not have been able to understand it at the time, but now that we're no longer children we can put what was happening into context.

What our parents and teachers were actually modelling for us was how adults in charge make rules for children, **not how adults make rules for other adults**. Formulating rules for other adults is in fact a different skill.

Unfortunately, many of the professionals who generate rules for other adults don't learn that skill first. As a result, too often we find policies saying "You must always do this," "We don't tolerate that," and "No exceptions will be made." As you hear the words in your head, you can almost see the finger wagging at you.

But is that condescending tone really what is intended?

In reality, in most cases the aggressiveness of the language isn't deliberate. The rule makers wanted to sound strict, not rude or disrespectful. They didn't realize they might sound like they're wagging their fingers at their employees or their customers.

What happens is that the people drafting the rules are so busy paying attention to content that they forget about tone of voice. It falls completely off the radar.

The Fallout

Dictating rules in an I-am-in-charge-and-you-will-obey-me tone of voice may or may not be appropriate for children. (I'm going to be non-partisan on that one; that's not my area of expertise.)

What I do know is that **to other adults, that tone of voice sounds disrespectful, and that disrespect — even if it's only heard subconsciously — gets people's backs up and engenders resentment.**

Compliance with rules is dependent upon people's coopera-tion. But we can't claim success if that "cooperation" is based solely on threats. **We want others to follow our rules willingly** — at best, cheerfully, at worst, begrudgingly. In either case, we won't get anywhere by antagonizing them.

If you want your employees to buy into your initiatives and to be on-side with you when you make changes, they need to want to support you. Employees who feel they've been spoken to in a disrespectful manner do not respond well. Unduly aggressive or dictatorial policies result in a loss of employee engagement. You see it in the form of compli-ance issues and high staff turnover.

The reaction is even more pronounced with customers; they won't tolerate it at all. If your customers don't like the way you speak to them, they turn away and don't come back.

At the end of the day, both employee turnover and customer dissatisfaction affect the bottom line: they drive your costs up and your revenues down.

Consistency with Other Values

The irony in this situation is that many of these organizations claim to have "respect for others" as a core value.

Many organizations genuinely respect their employees. They might even have taken steps to demonstrate that respect: building a nice staff lunchroom, or providing comfortable chairs or top-of-the-line technology. A few companies go so far as to take the time and effort to choose the right paint colour for the walls, to create a specific atmosphere.

But these same organizations don't look carefully at how their administrative and operational policies are worded. As a result, any negative messages conveyed along with that wording go unchecked. You can be sure that if their policies sound disrespectful to employees, the poor wording packs a lot more punch than having the wrong colour on the walls.

Rethinking the Wording of Rules

The good news is that this problem is relatively easy to fix if you want to. It requires learning only two things:

(a) how to recognize rules that sound disrespectful, and

(b) how to revise them so they don't.

That's all. We just have to want to. **We simply have to make communicating respectfully and courteously one of our priorities.**

This book is about drafting operational and administrative policies and similar types of rules documents in a way that's **clear**, **succinct**, and **respectful**.

I'm not going to challenge the content of your rules. If you believe a specific rule is required to bring you closer to your objectives, then for our purposes that justification is sufficient.

Nor will I be looking at the policy-making machine. We're not going to look at how to determine what the right rule is, how to run a consultation, or what makes a good approval process. All of that work is input into the **drafting process**, which is when the policy writers take up the reins.

The writers need to organize documents to hold the rules and generate the statements to assert them. This book will ask you to rethink how you approach those activities, as well as the way you address the people those rules are intended to govern.

You will begin to see that **the wording of your rules reveals the amount of respect** you have for the people they are directed to — or betrays the lack of it.

The Contents of This Book

This book moves from the more general to the more specific.

In Chapter 1, we'll look at the costs to your organization of poorly-written policies. We'll also look at why policies differ from contracts and how that difference is reflected in the wording.

Chapter 2 covers the drivers for policy writing. It looks first at why we make rules and then at why we write them down.

Chapter 3 deals with how to organize policy instruments and the importance of a documentation framework, and Chapter 4 looks at the naming of policy documents.

In Chapter 5, we start to examine the wording of policy statements. We concentrate here on making the wording clear and succinct. In Chapter 6, we look at making it sound respectful, and in Chapter 7 we take the initiative even further, to make the wording sound helpful.

Chapter 8 is devoted entirely to a discussion of the three modals, "must," "may," and "should." We'll see why these terms are both antiquated and terribly ambiguous, and we'll look at alternative wordings.

Chapter 9 focuses on a special type of policy instrument, the standard. We'll look at how standards differ from and interact with other types of policy instruments.

Chapter 10 focuses on another special type of policy instrument, the code of conduct. We'll look at how the drafting principles that make policy statements more engaging can do the same thing for codes of conduct.

In Chapter 11, we'll cover the elements that package policy statements, such as the tombstone information, the policy objective, and an enquiries statement.

Chapter 12 provides some drafting tips to help keep your policy statements clear, succinct, and respectful. We'll look at a number of commonly used words that are problematic.

The Examples

Most of the examples included in this book are pulled from real documents that have come across my desk. Though I normally like to give credit where credit is due, in this case the names of the organizations have all been hidden to avoid embarrassing anyone.

Still, I would like to express my deepest appreciation to those organizations for unknowingly contributing their bad policy statements as shining examples of what not to do. Without them, this book would not have been possible.

Chapter 1

THE COSTS OF BAD RULES

Karen tells me that whenever she's a candidate for a job, she asks to see the organization's corporate policies. She wants to know how the management speaks to employees. If she finds the language lacking respect, she quietly moves on to the next opportunity.

Good employees are hard to find. Someone who cares enough about her employment situation to do her due diligence around a candidate organization is exactly the kind of employee you want.

But you will lose Karen by not paying attention to this issue. Moreover, you will lose her without ever knowing it ... without knowing she came to peer into your window, didn't like what she saw, and then turned away.

How many Karens have looked at your organization's written policies and seen that they don't address others respectfully? How many Karens might you have missed out on until now?

Of course, we can never know that number, but if Karen is the right person for your organization then even one is too many. Our only hope is to take steps to prevent it from happening in the first place. We need policies that will sound respectful both to insiders and to outsiders.

Administrative and Operational Rules

"Policy," like many English words, has a variety of meanings.

On one end of the spectrum, it is used in the broad sense to refer to an overall political strategy, such as a policy on inflation or a country's foreign policy. On the other end, it refers to one specific rule, such as a "cash purchases only" policy.

This book is about your organization's **administrative and operational policies**. These are the decisions regulating the behaviour of others, be they employees of an organization, members of an association, or clients of a service you provide. Included are all services for corporate support — finance, human resources (HR), information management / information technology (IM/IT), security, facilities — and all day-to-day operations.

From this point on, we will restrict our discussion to that world.

The Old Way

Years ago I led a corporate services support team in a large government agency. The team members were constantly frustrated with the colleagues they supported. The team had previously published a series of policies and directives containing all the rules they wanted everyone to follow, but no one appeared to be listening.

At first, the team speculated that non-compliance was the result of poor communications, so it created more memoranda, posted announcements on the corporate intranet, and sent out e-mail reminders. But nothing changed; increased communications didn't inspire anyone to be more compliant.

Then the team tried beefing up the language to sound scarier and more official. It replaced the familiar opening gambit "Employees should " with the tougher-sounding "All employees must " and "All users are required to."

Finally, it added lots of **heavy boldface**, *italics*, <u>underline</u>, UPPERCASE LETTERS, and lots of exclamation marks(!!!!) to ***<u>make sure EVERYONE obeyed the rules!!!!</u>***

As you might suspect, the formatting changes did nothing to increase compliance. Somehow, people must have missed the memo explaining that the more formatting a rule has, the more it is supposed to cause you to shake in your boots.

The threatening wording also had no effect. If anything, it engendered resentment in some corners and caused friction between the policy writers and the rest of the office.

As you might expect, almost no one actually ever read the policies. Those who did read them were

+ confused about what they meant
+ reluctant to wade through numerous and unnecessarily lengthy paragraphs

+ disinclined to be open to the rules given the increasingly confrontational tone.

As it became clear that the new policy instruments were no more successful than the old ones, things went from bad to worse. The policy owners grew disillusioned.

"Why should we bother writing more policies if nobody's going to follow them?" team members would ask. "We're just wasting our time."

The team's morale dropped, its frustration level increased, and its productivity decreased.

The real problem was never addressed — namely, that the purpose of policy instruments was generally misunderstood. Newer policies were always based on older policies, despite the fact that the older policies might not have been written properly in the first place.

The Three Common Gremlins

Most written policies, directives, standards, and similar regulatory documents are plagued with three common gremlins.

1. Lack of clarity

The statements are ambiguous or confusing. Poorly-chosen wording permits multiple interpretations.

2. Lack of conciseness

Policy statements are interwoven with all kinds of tangentially relevant information, thereby failing to separate policy from explanation or advice. Documents are not concise because they try to do too many things at the same time.

3. Lack of respect

The policy statements sound like a sergeant barking orders. They admonish instead of inform.

Benefits of Well-Written Policies

Well-drafted policy statements invite compliance. They are easier to administer and enforce, reducing the amount of time the organization spends on those activities. They also make the internal audit process easier because the auditors can figure out exactly what the expected results are.

Well-drafted policy instruments can shorten the approval process by weeks or even months by containing only those statements that actually need to be approved.

Well-drafted policy instruments can more easily be navigated, maintained, and retired, as necessary.

The less time required to deal with issues caused by poor drafting, the more resources available to devote to the organization's main business.

Policies Versus Contracts

When I went to law school, the topic of corporate policies came up only sporadically and we learned nothing about policies and procedures outside of their legal implications. When I practised law, policies were treated simply as extensions to the contractual documentation.

It was only when I moved out of law and into the business world that I learned policies were a lot more than that.

Today, I run workshops on policy drafting and spend much of my time teaching professionals how to draft rules that don't sound overbearing or aggressive. Interestingly, whenever I get pushback on that approach, it invariably turns out the objection comes from a lawyer.

Many lawyers, of course, have no problem with policy documents sounding more engaging and less confrontational than they have historically. But some are not convinced; they want policies to sound strict, to convince us they mean business! In essence, they want policies to sound like contracts.

I get that. I get that their interest in the policies is limited to legal issues. But policies are not simply documents setting out terms and conditions. They have implications for the leadership style, management practices, corporate culture, and workplace wellness issues that define an organization.

Policies and contracts have different purposes. **The goal of a contract is to set out the agreed rights and obligations of the parties. The goal of a policy is to help the organization function properly.**

Contracts are drawn up to protect the parties. An employment contract sets out the terms of employment, and in theory protects both the employer and the employee. (In practise, though, it is usually drafted to protect only the employer.)

The primary concern when drafting contracts is **legal defensibility**. We don't care whether the people on the other side are positively engaged or feel warm fuzzies when reading it. We don't care whether they buy in emotionally to our approach. If the contract contains cold, strict-sounding language, so be it.

Policies are different. **We want our policies to encourage buy-in and induce compliance, and not to cause others to put their defences up.**

Well-written policies set a positive tone for the organization. They contribute to the ongoing **employee experience** long after the initial employment contract is signed. Similarly, customer policies contribute to a customer's experience long after the initial sale or service.

When you draft a policy as if it were a contract, you're missing out on an opportunity. Instead of improving engagement, it will engender resistance. Ignoring the human relations elements can prove **toxic to the corporate culture** and damaging to productivity.

Policy drafters need to work together with legal professionals, but each in their own spheres. We don't want our policies to be drafted exclusively by lawyers any more than we want our contracts to be drafted exclusively by policy writers.

The lawyers and the various subject matter experts in the organization are most likely on the same page when it comes to the outcomes they want to see. But their methodologies differ. The legal system is still primarily adversarial in approach; an organization's policy regime is collaborative.

I recommend that you pass all draft corporate policies through the legal department for an opinion. Lawyers can tell you about any risks stemming from what you put in the document. Once you understand those risks, you can decide if your policies are creating any risk you are unwilling to accept.

But stand your ground when it comes to regulating the tone of voice in the document. That tone of voice will have repercussions for you down the road, as you work with your colleagues.

Summary

Well-drafted policies invite compliance. If a few small changes to our documents will have a large effect, wouldn't it be worth the taking the time to do that?

Chapter 2

POLICY BASICS

Rules originate from multiple sources. We receive them from our caretakers, from government authorities, and from our religious beliefs, just to name a few. It would be impossible to produce an exhaustive inventory of the rules imposed on our lives even if we wanted to. Every formal and informal organization we interact with has its own rules.

As we grow up, we may choose to follow rules to a greater or lesser degree, depending on our character and our set of personal values. This is especially true when the rules coming from different sources conflict with one another. In those cases we have to make value judgments to choose among them.

Written Rules

Not all rules are written down, of course. Some are formed by habit or culture and exist as part of our normal social interaction as human beings.

Rules can remain unwritten so long as we want to preserve the status quo. But keeping our rules unwritten can be insufficient when we want to change behaviours. In those circumstances, we often need to formalize the rule, record it, and communicate it before we will see it take effect.

Rules in the Business World

I said earlier that most of us want to do the right thing at work. It's more than simply wanting to keep our jobs by pleasing our bosses. We genuinely want to serve our customers well, to help our colleagues, and to support those who report to us. In addition, we want to be productive, effective, and efficient.

Typically, the driver for rules in an organization is some *bona fide* organizational goal. Strategies are put into place to achieve specific objectives, and one output of the strategies is a set of rules.

In a formally structured organization, such as a business or government setting, the wide range of objectives leads to an even wider range of rules. Here are some examples of typical corporate objectives and the topics of the rules that might be drafted to support them.

1) Objective: keeping better track of our expenditures
   + formalizing our approval procedures
   + organizing the way we classify expenditures
   + changing the contents of financial reports

2) Objective: solidifying our marketing and branding
   + unifying the image we present to the public
   + controlling the language we use in our promotional material
   + defining target audiences and a sales process

3) Objective: improving customer satisfaction

+ maintaining standards around product quality

+ offering refunds and exchanges

+ supporting new activities and new roles for employees

4) Objective: reducing overhead costs

+ standardizing technology and components

+ reallocating job responsibilities

+ streamlining processes

Where a rule exists in a vacuum, without a clear objective behind it, many individuals will be reluctant to follow it. Business leaders are well aware of that tendency, and respond by making sure that at some point they communicate the "why" behind the "what." Once people understand the objective, they are more open to following the rule.

Rules Set a Dividing Line

Rules are valuable when they help us distinguish acceptable from unacceptable actions. Effectively, they draw a line in the sand and tell us one side is good and the other is bad. Crossing to the bad side will get us in trouble.

Whenever a decision comes down from on high that the right side is good and the left side is bad, we need to convey that rule. It can be worded in many ways, as illustrated by the examples in panel 2.

Panel 2

The right side is good and the left side is bad.

Keep to the right side.

Stay off the left side.

People must never, ever go to the left side.

The left side is forbidden.

People found on the left side will be shot.

Please do us a favour and stay on the right side.

In our office we stick to the right side.

And the list goes on.

There's no question that it's often critical to draw this line in the sand. If you want to discipline or fire an employee, kick someone out of a club, fine a tenant for breach of the rules, deny a service or benefit to a member of the public, and so on, the line between right and wrong has to be clear for all to see.

Why Write Rules Down

I said earlier that rules are formalized, then recorded, then communicated.

At the risk of stating the obvious, I'd like to point out that rules are not particularly useful if they are conveyed only through media having no permanence. Our ancestors may have been able to rely on oral tradition around the campfire to pass down rules from one generation to another, but it falls short of good business practice today.

Rules need to be written down for two simple reasons.

+ With only our memories to rely on, each of us would "know" only our own version of each rule.

+ With nothing written down, we have no solid evidence that the correct rule was communicated to those who need to follow it.

Forgive my contorting an old expression, but the truth is that **an unwritten rule isn't worth the paper it isn't written on**.

Writing rules down establishes two elements critical to good policy documents: **certainty** and **authority**.

1. Certainty

We need a common songbook if we're all going to sing together. As we each point to the governing paragraph, all fingers should be pointing to the same spot.

We need to know exactly what words the policy used, in what order, and with what punctuation. If we're all going to be on the same page, that page needs to be clearly identifiable and accurately reproducible.

Along with that certainty come consistency, durability, permanence, and all the other benefits of committing something to written form.

2. Authority

A rule is approved by a person or body. This approval conveys two critical pieces of information:

A) Provenance

The person or body approving the statement self-identifies and takes responsibility for the decision. If you are unhappy with the rule and want it to change or to go away, you need to convince that person or body.

By approving a written policy the approver is basically saying to the world, to put it colloquially, "The buck stops here. We have the authority to make this decision and it need go no higher."

B) Jurisdiction

Implicit in that approval is the additional assertion that the statements in the policy are within the scope of what that person or body can approve. Again, to put it colloquially, it announces, "This issue is ours to control."

To leverage a legal term, the approval of the policy is an assertion that the subject matter is within the **competence** of the approver.

"Competence" used in this sense is not about skills but rather about jurisdiction. Decisions you make over areas outside your competence are ineffective. Drafting them and submitting them for approval is a waste of your time and resources.

You might think the previous sentence states the obvious, but the evidence indicates otherwise. Many, many policies contain statements outside the competence of the approver, yet someone insists on including them nonetheless. We will examine this issue in more detail in Chapter 5.

Critical Statements Only

As a practical matter, obtaining approval for an operational or administrative policy can be an arduous and lengthy process. Every single statement appearing in the document has the potential to serve as a stumbling block should someone object to the way it's worded. The fewer stumbling blocks presented, the faster the policy will progress towards approval.

The *raison d'être* of a policy is to substantiate the two elements discussed above: certainty and authority. **If the policy is to be as concise as possible, it will contain only statements establishing certainty, authority, or both.**

Statements inserted for any other purpose are unnecessary. Unnecessary, in this situation, also means time-consuming and costly. It means chewing up the resources of the policy drafters, the people being consulted, the approvers, and everyone else involved in the policy process.

The test: if a statement would be just as **functional** were it to appear in another document — for example, a training document or a user guide — then that statement is dispensable.

In most organizations those other documents can be produced without the need for a full consultation and approval process. That being the case, **moving a dispensable statement out of the policy and into those other documents whenever possible will save you time and resources.**

Misguided Goals

The "other purposes" used to justify including dispensable statements fall into a few groups. You can tell what's really driving the inclusion by listening for clues in the justification. Here are examples of clues for each of these other purposes.

Clues

"People need to know this information."

"We want to remind people about this."

"We want everyone to know where this rule comes from."

Reality

Those kinds of explanations are signs a statement is being inserted into the policy for **educational** purposes.

We can educate people using other types of formats: instructional material, promotional material, live training, and so on, all falling under the general category of guidance.

Educational statements belong in the office manual; in a policy, they serve only as clutter.

Clues

"Some people won't understand it unless we expand on it more."

"We should probably give some examples to help people understand."

Reality

We can provide valid explanations and illustrations outside the policy document, in the same instructional material, promotional material, and live training mentioned above.

Which process is more time-consuming in your organization: getting a policy approved or getting instructional material approved? In most organizations the policy needs to go higher up, and that involves more steps and check-points than almost any other process. Save the policy work for the statements that have no choice but to go through that approval process, and put the other statements somewhere that involves less work.

Clues

"We want everyone to understand why the rule is this way."

"The approvers will want to know our rationale."

Reality

We can justify our rules by using other documents, such as strategy papers, reports, and information sessions.

When a bill goes before an elected government body for approval, the bill itself does not contain the justification for its existence. Any background information, justification, or supporting evidence comes in a **separate document accompanying** the bill. Once the bill is passed into law, that supporting document is moved somewhere else, and the statute or by-law that's left contains only the rules.

Draft policies are the corporate equivalent to those bills. If the justification for the rules changes, you don't want to have to amend your policies just to update the justification! Keep those documents separate.

Clues

"We need to cover all the angles."

"People will want to know everything."

Reality

A good policy does not have to be a compendium of everything to know on a given subject.

An organization will have lots of documentation explaining who, what, where, when, and how, to those who need to know. This topic will be discussed more fully in the next chapter, where I group all the documents supporting the policies under the collective heading "office manual."

A good office manual tells workers in the organization everything they need to know. A good office manual can educate, explain, provide examples and illustrations, and communicate the justification for why the rule is the way it is.

We want our office manuals to be as comprehensive as possible, whereas we want our policies to be as succinct as possible.

Adding statements to your policies that educate, explain, or justify the rules effectively turns your policies into an office manual.

The ultimate test? **If omitting a statement does not alter the rule, the statement belongs somewhere else.**

Terminology

Because policy-making terminology varies from discipline to discipline, misunderstandings are common. In this book, I have tried to be consistent with the following terms:

A **policy decision** is a decision adopted by a governing body in the organization. (We will refine this statement later, but for now it's sufficient for our purposes.)

A **policy statement** is a written declaration of that decision.

A **policy instrument** is a document containing one or more policy statements.

The governing body approving the policy instrument becomes the **owner** of that policy. The policy may have been drafted by subject matter experts, and then may undergo a series of consultations, reiterations, and interim approvals, but eventually the document is submitted to the policy owner for final approval.

For our purposes, **the policy owner is the decision-making person or body whose approval actually puts the policy into effect.**

An individual or body acquires the authority to approve a policy from one of several sources:

+ It may be born of a constitutional document, such as a charter or a government law or regulation.
+ It may be declared in a management document, such as corporate by-laws or an internal governance framework.
+ It may result from a delegation, which is the formal assignment by a higher power of the right to make a decision.
+ It may arise simply through one's ownership or sponsorship of the organization. As my father used to say, "The man who pays the piper calls the tune."

The policy owner is ultimately responsible for the policy decisions.

Summary

Trying to make a single document serve all purposes creates a monster. Many policy documents could be cut to half their current length if their contents were limited to policy statements.

Now let's turn to look at the different kinds of documents these policy owners produce.

Chapter 3

POLICY INSTRUMENTS

It was not long after my engagement as the policy specialist in a mid-size, think-tank–type organization that somebody sent me a document to look over. He had put together a short piece titled *Guidelines on Visitor Security* that he wanted to distribute to the rest of the organization, and asked me to provide feedback on its content.

I started to read it. The preamble was overly long and not particularly informative. It looked like it had been copied from another corporate policy instrument and amended by using the word "visitor" to replace what might have been "cell phones" in the original. I slid over the preamble and moved directly to the policy statements.

The first statement is set out in panel 3.

Panel 3

A "visitor" is someone who does not work in our organization.

Interesting start. I would have thought that fact to be self-evident, but I guess the writer was erring on the side of caution. The definition wasn't wrong, so not a big deal.... Moving on.

The second statement can be seen in panel 4.

Panel 4

All visitors must be escorted by an employee while they are on the premises.

Okay. The intent was clear, even though I might have worded it a little more succinctly and a lot less dictatorially. But if that statement represents the position the organization wants to take, then it is appropriate for the statement to appear in a policy instrument.

Panel 5 contains the third statement.

Panel 5

Please tell your visitors to arrive ten minutes prior to the appointment to register with the security desk.

Pardon me?

This statement suggests our official organizational policy is to tell visitors to arrive ten minutes early. It didn't sound like a decision made by a high-level executive committee; it sounded more like advice you might give new colleagues when orienting them to the office. It was not insignificant that the statement began with "please," a word much out of place in a policy decision.

From there, things continued to go downhill. The fourth statement appears in panel 6.

Panel 6

> Visitors are expected to behave appropriately at all times.

Whoa! Seriously?

If this is supposed to be a statement of a decision, what were they deciding? Doesn't this sentence state the obvious? Did we really need the most senior-ranking officials at the organization to spend their time approving this statement?

Leaving aside for the moment the possibility that we may not all agree on what constitutes "appropriately," this statement suffers from a serious clarity problem due to the word "expected." On its face, it's not a statement about reasonable behaviour; it's a statement about reasonable expectations around behaviour.

Was this wording chosen to avoid saying "visitors must behave"? That's most likely what they want. This statement might be useful on a sign in the visitors' waiting area, but it's not a statement of policy.

The fifth statement was even worse. It's set out in panel 7.

Panel 7

> As stated in the office security policy, visitors must wear an identification badge at all times.

It seems we already have a policy telling visitors to wear an identification badge, but now someone wants a new policy telling everyone to follow the existing policy. It's as if someone is trying to think up some rules solely to bulk up the document.

I stopped reading and put the document down. It was a dog's breakfast of general advice, best practices, definitions, new policy statements, and reminders about existing policy statements.

Separating Rules from Guidance

I went back to the person who sent me the document and asked the question I now pose immediately upon receiving a document for review: Is this document intended to be an authority or is it intended to be guidance?

Put differently, is the purpose of this document

- to set out decisions that a governing body needs to approve, or
- to inform people in the office of what they need to know about the subject?

Those are two separate kinds of documents. The first is a policy, the second is guidance.

A fundamental distinction exists between documents that set rules and documents that restate or explain them. The critical flaw in the policy instruments of most organizations is the failure to preserve this distinction.

Documentation Framework

The documents related to policies in an organization fall into one of three groups. Together these three groups comprise the organization's **policy documentation framework.** (See Figure 1.)

These three sets of documents are

+ foundational documents
+ authorities
+ guidance

The small arrows leading from one section to another mean "inform." Foundational documents inform the authorities, and those in turn inform the guidance documents.

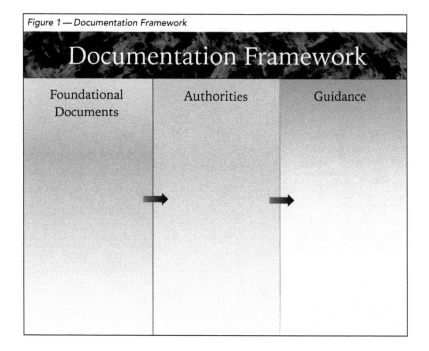

Figure 1 — Documentation Framework

Documentation Framework

| Foundational Documents | Authorities | Guidance |

Let's explore each group separately.

Foundational Documents

Before you ever put pen to paper to draft policies, you most likely have created a number of documents around the direction of your organization. (See Figure 2.)

Foundational documents include

+ mandate documents
+ vision statements and mission statements
+ corporate values
+ goals and targets
+ operational measures and key performance indicators

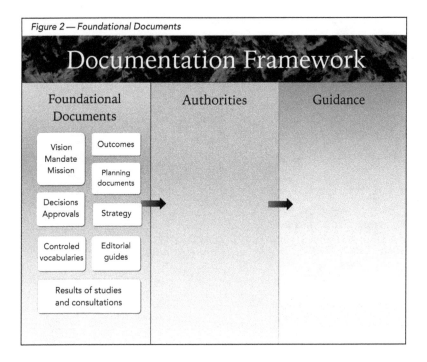

Figure 2 — Foundational Documents

- research and white papers
- strategies
- terminology lexicons

Foundational documents reflect the thinking done before the policies are created. They also include documents produced during the policy development process, such as records of discussions and the results of consultations. Have you heard of evidence-based policy writing? Those foundational documents are the evidence.

Foundational documents are amended infrequently, but it does happen. Because foundational documents inform the authorities, amendments to the former often require consequential changes to the latter.

Authorities

The second group of documents is the authorities. These are the various instruments setting the rules to be followed.

Authorities are either **internal** or **external** in origin.

Internal authorities include policies, directives, standards, and the other rules documents you develop. (See Figure 3.)

The owners of these authorities — individuals and committees — sit at a high level in the organization.

External authorities are those created by other bodies, both

- those you are obliged to follow, such as government legislation and professional regulation, and

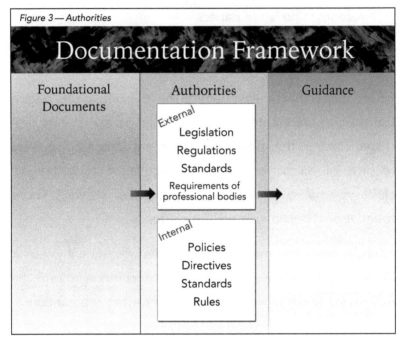

Figure 3 — Authorities

Documentation Framework

Foundational Documents | Authorities | Guidance

External
Legislation
Regulations
Standards
Requirements of professional bodies

Internal
Policies
Directives
Standards
Rules

✦ those you choose to follow, such as industry or international standards.

Both internal and external authorities can inform guidance documents. But unlike your internal authorities, the external ones are not informed by your foundational documents.

Creating and modifying authorities is a significant undertaking. A mature organization will have a documented, structured formal process to take its authorities through various stages, from draft to approval. In many cases the rigour of that process is compounded by the difficulty in obtaining the time or attention of the policy owners or the stakeholders.

As a result, producing, amending, or rescinding an authority is often intensely time- and resource-consuming. The most cost-effective way to speed up the process is to develop the initial draft in a way that requires as few changes as possible.

Guidance

This group contains the tools and guidance documents you create. These documents present, explain, and expand on all the information people need to know about the authorities. (See Figure 4.)

It is these documents that speak directly to those who are governed by the policies. They are effective only when they are written in plain language and are easy to navigate.

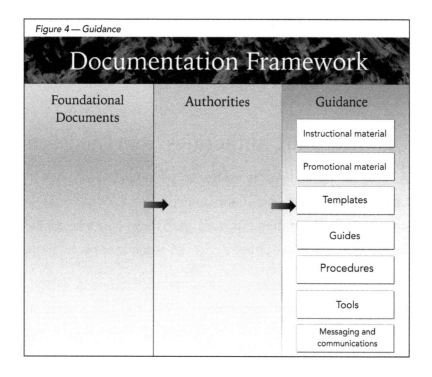

Figure 4 — Guidance

Documentation Framework

Foundational Documents	Authorities	Guidance
		Instructional material
		Promotional material
		Templates
		Guides
		Procedures
		Tools
		Messaging and communications

Guidance may be tailored specifically to different audiences, with some materials directed to management and others to rank-and-file employees. It may be reproduced in multiple publication formats, various levels of granularity, or even translated into different languages.

Since guidance documents are informed by the authorities, the guidance is correct only so long as it doesn't contradict an authority. You can keep your guidance current and accurate by setting up a process whereby changes to any policy instrument are followed by a review of the associated sections in the office manual.

Most organizations find it more efficient to permit the guidance documents to be approved at a level lower than the policy owner. The lower approval level gives the organization the flexibility it needs to produce support documentation more quickly and with fewer bureaucratic stumbling blocks.

Distinguishing Authorities from Guidance

As mentioned earlier, the failure to preserve the distinction between column 2 documents and column 3 documents — between policy statements and guidance — is the critical flaw in the policy instruments of most organizations.

The distinction is not new by any means. Librarians, historians, researchers, and archeologists call the documents in column 2 "primary sources" to distinguish them from those in column 3, which they call "secondary sources." Lawyers make a similar distinction, referring to the documents in column 2 as "law" and those in column 3 as "legal authorities" or "legal commentators."

The distinction is fundamental: **authorities set the rules, guidance restates them.**

Who Reads the Policies?

Too often I hear subject matter professionals complain about this issue. "Nobody is reading our *Policy on Paper Clips*," they lament. (In place of paper clips, feel free to insert a topic from your own domain: finance, IM/IT, security, HR, and so on.)

"Our organization ought to **force** everybody to read our paper clip policy," they continue, "so they will know all about our paper-clipping requirements."

My response is always the same:

1. Given the choice, 99% of the people in your organization will never read your paper clip policy.
2. Get used to it. That is not going to change.
3. It's not a bad thing.

"But they are governed by that policy!" they counter. "If it applies to them, then they should have to read it."

That last statement is a bit of a leap in logic. Let's put the shoe on the other foot for a moment.

The Income Tax Act

Did you file an income tax return last year? You may have filled out the return yourself, or you might have asked someone to do that for you. Whichever it was, tell me: did you first read the relevant *Income Tax Act*?

After all, **the *Income Tax Act* is the authority.** It lays out the rules and governs what you need to report in your return. It clearly does apply to you, so by the logic above you ought to have read it at least once!

Reality check: unless you're a tax lawyer or accountant, I'd be surprised if you'd ever even skimmed through that act, much less read it before filling out your tax form.

If you do read any tax-related document, it's most likely to be the little booklet accompanying the tax form, called something like *Instructions for Filling Out Your Tax Return*. That booklet is **guidance.** Its purpose is to provide you with only the information you need to be able to complete the task at hand, and for that reason people are far more likely to read that booklet than the Act itself. The booklet won't overload your brain by discussing parts of the legislation you don't need to know.

I doubt you're ever going to want to read the *Income Tax Act*. The government doesn't expect you to read it, nor do the tax experts you hire to help you. You may be governed by it, but that's not a sufficient reason for you to crack it open.

Getting Help

Working on your return, when you come across something you don't understand in that little booklet, you're *still* not going to reach for the *Income Tax Act* to help you out, even if it is the authoritative document. Instead, you will find someone to ask, like a friend, colleague, or tax professional.

The reality is that no one wants to read your *Policy on Paper Clips* any more than you want to read the *Income Tax Act*.

The reason is simple: when you aren't an expert in a field, you do not believe reading the authoritative document will be a good use of your time.

People Read Guidance

People are far more likely to read documents written specifically to help them do their jobs, like the little income tax form booklet.

If you can provide good documentation, explaining only what people need to know in a given situation, they will be far more receptive to reading that. After reading that, if they still have questions, they will contact you for an explanation before they ever reach for the authority.

Many parts of our lives work that way. You may have played Monopoly® numerous times, but it's unlikely that you've pored through the official rules from Hasbro (or the original ones from Parker Brothers). You can chair a meeting without ever reviewing *Roberts' Rules of Order*. And you can learn to drive your car without reading the applicable motor vehicle legislation.

Authorities are go-to materials when you need to settle a dispute. It's the same as how you use a dictionary, reaching for it to help work through a specific situation rather than reading it through from start to finish.

Policy Instruments Are for Experts

The *Income Tax Act* contains a lot of technical language. So does *Robert's Rules of Order*.

Like all good authorities, they are written for **accuracy** and **precision**, not to be educational tools. There is no expectation that an individual unfamiliar with the field should be able to pick up the authority and immediately understand it. While a large number of people may be governed by a policy or standard, a much smaller number will ever read it.

Too often, a policy is "dumbed down" because of the fear that some individual, some day, somewhere, may read the document and not understand the terminology. That fear raises calls to re-draft the text into everyday language.

The assumption driving that language simplification is that everyone is supposed to be able to understand a policy. That assumption is incorrect. It is based on the failure to distinguish the purpose of policy instruments from the purpose of guidance documents.

Authorities are not written for the layperson. Authorities are written using language the **experts who work in that field** can understand.

First and foremost, it is the experts in the field who need to be able to agree on what the policy statements mean, what the decisions are, and where the lines are being drawn. They need to agree whether left or right is good or bad. It is these individuals who will write the guidance that everyone else can read.

Let's look at an example. A local hospital has the policy shown in panel 8.

Panel 8

All incoming cases presenting sub-dermal or sub-cutaneous lesions are treated as epidemiological risks.

I have no clue what that policy means.

But so what? Whether I understand that policy has no bearing on anything. I'm not a medical specialist; I'm a patient. If I'm supposed to take some action based on this policy, a sign will be posted somewhere in plain language telling me to wash my hands or wear ugly cloth slippers or whatever it is I'm supposed to do.

Truth be told, even if they rewrote their policy in lay terms, I still wouldn't read it. If they want me to follow some rules, they will hand me a pamphlet called Information for Patients. That pamphlet needs to be in plain language so I can understand it, but the policies informing it can be as technical as they need to be.

What's important is that the medical specialists are all in agreement on what the policy means. If they agree on what it means, then they can explain it to the rest of us.

On the other hand, if they don't all agree on what it means, then we have a problem worth paying attention to! That problem needs to be fixed before going any further.

When drafting a policy statement, it's difficult enough to obtain agreement among the experts in that field. Far too often, if you dig a bit, you'll find that all the experts in an organization don't agree on what the policy statement means. That situation is a recipe for disaster.

If you can achieve a single, common understanding of a given wording among the experts, you have done as much as can be expected. It is onerous and unnecessary to impose the additional requirement that non-experts need to understand it. **Provide the non-experts with good guidance documents and they won't ever need to read the policy instruments.** The guidance will tell them everything they need to know.

Keep the Policy in Your Back Pocket

A policy instrument is like a wall stud rather than the wall itself. It supports the wall, but it shouldn't be visible when you walk into the room.

If the guidance is well written, most people never have to see the authority. The only time anyone will need to produce the actual policy instrument is when we need to check it in the context of a problem. Like the dictionary, we can turn to it when needed.

On rare occasions, someone will come to you to challenge a statement in the guidance. They're upset, for example, that the office manual says they can't chew bubble gum while working at the service counter. They storm into your office shouting, "Show me! Show me where it says that in the policy!"

On those occasions, you will be prepared. You calmly reach into your back pocket — figurative speaking — and pull out the policy instrument. You point to the appropriate statement and softly say, "See right here? Where it says 'no masticatory substances'? That means bubble gum."

Apart from that situation, most people need never read the actual policy, much less understand it.

Summary

1. Given the choice, 99% of the people in your organization will never read your paper clip policy.

2. Get used to it. That is not going to change.

3. It's not a bad thing.

Chapter 4

ORGANIZING AUTHORITIES

Your individual rules need to be bundled and organized into a variety of policy instruments. Let's look at how best to do that.

Instrument Titles

A number of possible document titles can be pressed into service, among them:

+ authority
+ catalogue
+ code
+ directive
+ guide
+ guideline
+ handbook
+ instructions
+ key
+ manual
+ matrix
+ obligation
+ policy
+ protocol
+ regulation
+ requirement
+ rule
+ scheme
+ specification
+ standard

The nuances differentiating these types of instruments may be subtle, but that's not really a problem for most organizations because they don't need to distinguish instruments to this level of granularity.

The International Standards Organization (ISO) endorses specific definitions for "policy," "procedure," and similar documents, but if your organization has not been using the terminology according to those definitions, I wouldn't lose sleep over it.

The title "standard" is reserved for documents of a specific nature. We'll look at those in Chapter 9.

The title "code" implies that the document is comprehensive, because an attempt was made to gather all the rules related to that subject in one single document, for example, a "building code" or a "code of conduct." (We'll look at codes of conduct in Chapter 10.)

Whether a "protocol" indicates an authority or a guidance document in your organization is really up to you. What matters is that **all documents titled the same way fall into the same group.** If the "Guideline on Contracting" is an authority but the "Guideline on Hiring" is just guidance, much confusion will ensue. What's important here is internal consistency.

Some organizations assign instrument titles to documents based on the different audiences they are written for. For example, "policy" might designate an authority directed at senior management while a "directive" is aimed at front-line workers.

Do what works for you, but always preserve the distinction between authorities and guidance. A document is one or the other: it either (1) sets rules or (2) restates or explains rules. **A single document cannot contain statements that belong to different groups.**

One Policy or Many?

Do we want to have one single big policy or a number of smaller ones? I hear this question debated a lot in the planning stages.

On the one side some people want a single all-inclusive totally comprehensive tome containing all the relevant statements on a particular subject and are not concerned that it might end up being extremely long and potentially overly complicated because at least it will put all the requirements relevant to a given subject in one place and give them to you in one breath just like this sentence.

In contrast, some people don't. They like to break the material up. They prefer multiple documents. Each document has its own subject. Each is short. Each is easy to read.

Which approach is better?

Applicability and Enforcement

When it comes to interpretation, applicability, and enforcement, the question is irrelevant. Totally irrelevant.

An old joke tells of a customer who orders a cherry pie. Before boxing it, the baker asks the customer whether it should be cut into six pieces or eight pieces. The customer responds, "Six pieces, please. I couldn't possibly eat eight pieces of pie."

What's important is that our policy documents are coherent, integrated, and uniformly structured; that individual policy statements do not conflict with one another; that we have eliminated duplication, and achieved clarity and succinctness. Those are all good goals.

At the end of the day we may find we have 400 unique policy statements. Whether we package those 400 statements into one, two, or 100 documents doesn't change the fact that we have 400 statements. If you wanted to, you could have 400 distinct documents, each with one statement, and you would still have exactly the same policy regime.

The number of documents has no influence on your ability to apply or enforce the provisions. However, it does have bearing on other aspects of the policy-drafting process.

Approving the Policy

When it comes to running the policy through an approval process, there's no question about it: **the larger the policy instrument, the longer it takes to get approved.** The more statements appearing in the document, the more points available to object to.

Smaller documents offer you some flexibility during the approval process. If you break your policy statements into ten documents, and there's a problem with a statement in one document, the other nine can still move ahead while you sort out the problem.

Organize what works for you. Some pieces of legislation, like the *Income Tax Act*, have thousands of paragraphs and sub-paragraphs. Some statutes contain only one single substantive provision. There's no reason an organizational policy can't be comprised of a single rule exactly the same way.

Let me pose the question this way: if we know a particular issue is likely to be a stumbling block for the approval committee, would we like that issue to hold up the entire policy, or just a piece of it?

I always go for the piecemeal approach in this case.

Navigating the Policy

Your strategy around the division of policy statements into different documents will affect discoverability. The question is totally practical: can those who will use them — mostly experts — find what they are looking for?

With 400 statements, you will want some system in place to pick out specific sections, no matter how many documents they are scattered through.

The more important concern is about the nature of the navigational tools you need to provide access to the policy instruments. Those tools need to be able to locate the right sections as quickly as possible.

Shedding the "Document" Model

In today's workplace, where most information is made available electronically, the concept of organizing policy statements in "documents" is somewhat anachronistic. A single 20-statement policy instrument can just as easily be displayed on five separate web pages with four statements each as it can be on a single web page.

Some organizations have done away with "policy documents" entirely, in favour of a **database of policy statements**. The statements get approved at different times and added to the database when appropriate. The database provides an easy search function for those seeking specific information.

If the explanation of a term can appear in a pop-up window, the reader really doesn't care whether that definition formed part of the original policy or was part of a different one — or even, for that matter, if it doesn't come from a policy at all but is provided simply to help.

Summary

How statements are grouped when submitted to the approving body is of no consequence to the reader. Presenting draft policy statements to an owner for approval and making approved statements accessible to a searcher are separate activities.

Chapter 5

POLICY STATEMENTS

In Chapter 2, I offered a cursory explanation of terms, characterizing a policy as a decision and a policy statement as a statement setting out that decision.

It's time to clarify what kind of decision constitutes a policy decision.

Decision Competence

As discussed in an earlier chapter, when a person or group in a position of power approves a policy document, implicit in that approval is the assertion that the issues decided are within the competence of the policy owner.

Most people recognize this issue in the most obvious of cases, but fail to spot it in more subtle cases.

Geographic Jurisdiction

Let's start with a ridiculously obvious case, to underscore the point.

Imagine that one of the state governments in the United States were to approve the policy in panel 9.

Panel 9

People living in Britain must wear hats at night.

It's absurd, of course. The government of one nation obviously has no legal authority to make rules binding the individuals of another. In the vocabulary of law-making, we would say that regulating the wearing of hats in Britain is outside the competence of a U.S. state government.

If someone doubted our determination about the limits of authority, we could support our position by identifying the specific body that **does have the competence** to make those rules if it wanted to, namely, Her Majesty's Government in London.

A Word on Enforceability

You might protest that the shortcoming of the hats-in-Britain policy is that it is unenforceable, but before you discount a rule on that basis you would be wise to answer two questions.

First, **what exactly is unenforceable about it?**

The "unenforceability" of a rule is not an objectively measurable state; rather, it is a conclusion to be reached after evaluating the circumstances.

Too often, rules are dismissed immediately as "unenforceable" the moment someone points out one of the following drawbacks:

* Infractions are difficult to detect.
* Infractions are difficult to prove.
* Infractions are not easily attributable to a specific source.
* Evidence of the infraction is perishable or transient.
* Enforcement mechanisms are not available.
* Enforcement mechanisms are ineffective.
* Enforcement mechanisms are too costly.
* Enforcement happens too late in the process to avoid the damage.

If you want to dismiss the rule in panel 9 as unenforceable, you need to pin down **exactly** what you think the roadblock is. It's not as simple as saying that the U.S. can't enforce a law in Britain, because British and U.S. law enforcement agencies cooperate very well when they need to.

Even if you find one or more of the above circumstances exists in the situation you're facing, that need not end the discussion. There may be work-arounds.

The second question is, **Does unenforceability *per se* invalidate the rule?**

Take, for instance, the first reason listed above — that infractions are difficult to detect. High-tech espionage is illegal despite any inherent detection difficulties. No one advocates that that law should come off the books until we come up with an easier way to expose spies. Even if infractions are difficult to detect today, they might not be tomorrow. The law stands, despite potential difficulties in enforcement.

For decades, governments resisted passing laws to control tobacco smoking in offices, restaurants, and public places, and always tendered the excuse that those laws would be "unenforceable." Yet today those laws exist in many jurisdictions. Why the change? It's not due to any amazing advances in our ability to detect smoke or to enforce laws. The only change was in people's attitudes.

The salient point is that the determination of competence is unrelated to issues around enforceability.

Assessing Competence

Geography imposes clear limits on the competence of a decision-making body.

Other limits on decision-making competence may not be as obvious. Panel 10 shows a statement extracted from an organization's employment policy.

Panel 10

Employees are forbidden from using illegal drugs.

That statement doesn't belong in an organization's employment policy — or any policy, for that matter.

Employees are already prohibited from using illegal drugs, by definition. Where government laws prohibit the use of a substance, an organization subject to those laws can't very well have rules contradicting them.

The legality of drugs falls within the competence of the government, and unless it has delegated powers down to your organization to make decisions in that regard, your organization doesn't have a say about it. The policy owner that approves this statement in an employment policy is purporting to make a decision outside its competence.

A statement restating an existing law or truth is not a policy decision. It belongs in the guidance.

Back to Basics

Some organizations defend including an illegal drugs statement in their own policy. Even when a rule is not their decision to make, they like to repeat existing laws and facts in their policies to highlight their existence or importance.

That approach might sound helpful, but at what cost?

Remember the distinction we made early on? **Authorities set rules; guidance restates them.** "Reminding" someone of the existence of a law or fact is part of the education process. We do not write policies in order to educate others. We write guidance to educate; **we write policies to set rules that don't yet exist.** Putting educational material into your policies blurs the line between authority and guidance.

The policy development process takes enough time already, without someone adding unnecessary work. Educational statements serve only to dilute policies with material that doesn't need to be drafted, considered, consulted on, approved, maintained ... and so on. Moving those statements to the guidance saves everyone time at every stage and results in a leaner product.

Restating Legislation

This drafting principle applies to all statements that simply restate an existing law. Each of the examples in panel 11 has little value as a policy decision.

Panel 11

Employees must handle all hazardous substances in accordance with existing laws and regulations.

All documents are subject to applicable freedom of information and privacy legislation.

All hiring must comply with the *Americans with Disabilities Act.*

In each of these examples, **the statement is true whether or not the organization adds it to a policy.** It doesn't become truer by appearing twice.

The organization's policy instruments lose their integrity when they make it look like others' decisions are their own. The organization didn't make the decisions in panel 11. Putting those statements inside corporate policy instruments **misrepresents the owner** of those statements, portraying the statements as corporate decisions when they are not.

That portrayal, aside from misrepresenting the truth, sends a self-aggrandizing message. It sounds like the organization is saying "We don't want you to abstain from illegal drugs at work because the government says so. We want you to do it **because we say so**. If we discipline you, it won't be because you broke the law, but because you disobeyed **us**."

All statements using the form "Employees must follow the law" have the same shortcoming: they are true whether or not your organization puts them into a policy.

Based on this discussion, we can refine our description of a policy as follows:

A policy is a decision

+ **within the competence of the policy owner**
+ **making something true that isn't yet true.**

That's the definition we will be using going forward.

Testing for Inclusion

The "hereby" construction is an easy way to check each proposed statement to help you determine whether it is within your competence.

Since a policy statement isn't true until that policy is approved, the **approval officially enacts the statement**. The approval functions as an on-switch, turning the statement from "not yet true" to "true from now on."

That enactment can be reflected by the word "hereby" or, depending on the context, the phrases "hereby confirmed," "hereby deemed," or "hereby considered."

Take the example in panel 12.

Panel 12

Working hours are from 9:00 AM to 5:00 PM.

Using the "hereby" test, we can generate the statement in panel 13.

Panel 13

Working hours are hereby deemed to be from 9:00 AM to 5:00 PM.

Of course, that wording sounds stiff and pretentious and you wouldn't write it that way. Still, the content is accurate.

Contrast that with the statement from the employment policy in panel 10, repeated for your convenience in panel 14.

Panel 14

Employees are forbidden from using illegal drugs.

Using the "hereby" test, that statement expands to the one in panel 15.

Panel 15

Employees are hereby forbidden from using illegal drugs.

In this case it's not just the pretentiousness that's objectionable. The statement is factually inaccurate. The policy is not enacting this rule; it has already been enacted somewhere else. If the statement can't stand as a "hereby" statement, then it's not actually making a decision. The "hereby" in panel 15 just accentuates the problem, making it easier for us to see.

Building on a Law

I'm not suggesting that any issues covered by legislation are off limits. A valid policy statement can **extend** or **supplement** an existing law.

Assume, for example, a municipality with a by-law limiting motor vehicle speed to 55 km/h (35 mph) on major roads. For liability reasons, a company with a fleet of trucks approves the policy shown in panel 16.

Panel 16

Company drivers on delivery runs do not exceed speeds of 40 km/h (25 mph).

This company policy doesn't restate or contradict the by-law; rather, it exacts an additional restriction. The policy is valid so long as the by-law doesn't prohibit that kind of restriction. Policy ownership is still represented accurately: the company is the owner of the statement containing the more restrictive speed limit.

Summary

When your policies contain only statements being enacted by the approval body, they will be leaner — free of the excess baggage bloating most instruments. You'll find that these leaner documents move through the stages of the development and approval processes at a much faster rate.

It's now time to turn our attention to an area that gets far too little attention in policy writing: the tone of voice.

Chapter 6

PROMOTING RESPECT

I kid you not. At the clinic where my doctor works, a sign hangs on the wall beside the reception desk, shouting the following warning:

> ## RUDE AND AGGRESSIVE BEHAVIOUR WILL NOT BE TOLERATED
>
> You will be asked to leave. If you do not leave, the authorities will be called. *No exceptions.*

Sitting in the reception area, you can't help but think to yourself, "Really? What goes on at this place that they need to talk to patients this way?"

The receptionists themselves are quite pleasant. I feel bad for them because the sign looms above them, suggesting they are ready to pounce on you for any mis-step. A lot of individuals are already nervous when they enter a doctor's office, and that sign in the waiting room doesn't calm them down.

My doctor is apologetic. The sign was posted by the clinic owner and is beyond his control. I personally raised the issue with the clinic supervisor, but even after three years the sign is still there.

As mentioned in the introduction to this book, many organizations claim to hold "respect for others" as a core value. They talk a good game, for sure, but do they practice what they preach?

Compare the A and B statements in panels 17 and 18.

Panel 17

A) All employees must start work every day by 9:00 and must leave the office no earlier than 17:00.

B) Working hours are from 9:00 to 17:00.

Panel 18

A) Employees must submit vacation requests at least one week in advance. Any request not submitted on time may be refused.

B) Requests for vacation are considered when submitted at least one week in advance.

Can you hear the difference in the tone of voice between the A and B statements?

The B statement in each case requires the same action from the employee as the A one but does not sound nearly as dictatorial.

Why is the A-type statement so common?

As alluded to in the Introduction, dictating rules in an "I-am-in-charge-and-you-will-obey-me" tone of voice is a product of a bygone era, when command-and-control organizational structures were considered the optimal approach to obtaining employee engagement.

Years ago, that authoritarian tone of voice was standard in communications coming from upper management to rank-and-file employees. Bosses spoke that way and they wrote that way. The language and style never raised an eyebrow; they were expected.

Today, things are different. Today's workplace is not the command-and-control autocracy it was in days past. Today's workplace is a collaborative, consensus-building, diversity-respecting, egalitarian, and non-discriminatory environment, where employers strive to create and maintain a culture of respect.

As part of this culture, progressive managers have learned to communicate more courteously to employees. Even the professionals who use overly authoritarian language in their written policies don't use that same wording when they speak directly to others in the organization.

Resulting from a Bad Experience

It's not hard to read between the lines in the two A statements above. This organization clearly has had some rough experiences with people not adhering to the prescribed office hours and failing to meet the notice period required for the making of vacation requests.

Look back at the A examples and see if you can detect the emotional undertones of the wording. They are subtle, but clearly perceptible. Try to imagine someone speaking those words aloud and listen carefully to the tone of voice.

Clearly, the office that produced the first statement of each pair is experiencing a compliance problem. Moreover, it sounds like those working in that office are frustrated by that problem and tired of reminding others about the policy.

We get it; we've all been there. We have all experienced administering a policy that someone doesn't follow for one reason or another.

But the rest of the world doesn't need to know that. If your policies are well written, you will look like you know what you're doing. If the wording of your policies exposes your compliance problems, you will be revealing much more than you need to.

We don't know the back story. The organization could be ex-periencing compliance problems. Alternatively, it's possible that someone feels the need to make dictatorial pronounce-ments to reinforce the pecking order in the office. Or maybe employees are always asking for exemptions and the writer is tired of saying no each time. Someone is frustrated, or tired, or high on a power trip, or all of those, and those emotions are reflected in the writing.

Ask yourself, is that the face of your organization you want outsiders to see? Wouldn't it be better if the policy statements were emotionally neutral?

Unintended Messages

Unintended messages are delivered through undertones, hidden between the lines. They can be negative messages, like these:

+ We're rigid.
+ We don't care if this is inconvenient.
+ We expect obedience.
+ We're watching you.

or positive messages, like these:

+ We're flexible.
+ We recognize that this is difficult.
+ We appreciate your cooperation.
+ We trust you to do the right thing.

As the person or organization behind the policy, it's difficult for you to hear the undertones of your own writing. The lens of your interpretation is from the back, where you're more concerned about content than style. Like watching a play, you can't see it properly if you're standing on the stage.

When you switch the lens to the front — from the viewpoint of someone subject to the policy — the messages get louder.

Take the example in panel 19.

Panel 19

> All employees must always check in at the front desk upon arrival.

Had the policy been written concisely, it would look like the one in panel 20.

Panel 20

> Employees check in at the front desk upon arrival.

So why the extra words — "all," "must," and "always" — in panel 19? Some writers claim that those words make the statement clearer. Perhaps, but they actually do more than that. Because they are superfluous, they are laden with hidden messages.

"all"

The word "all" is implied; without it the statement means the same. Its deliberate inclusion here reveals a specific underlying sentiment, along the lines of "We don't care about individual circumstances."

"must"

The word "must" is overkill; it's a glove slapping your face. Its inclusion here says, "Yes, this is mandatory. You need to obey us."

"always"

The word "always" is another loaded word. Again, the statement would mean the same without it. Its inclusion here says, "We're not flexible. Don't even think about asking to be an exception."

Unless these are messages you truly want to send, it would be better to rewrite the policy statement.

Well-Worded Policy Statements

The archetypal policy statement is found in panel 21.

Panel 21

Business hours run from 9:00 A.M. to 5:00 P.M.

It is a declarative sentence in the present tense. It describes, in a neutral voice, the way things are as a matter of course. It's just "how we operate around here."

The simple present tense in policy statements works well because it can be used to complete a sentence beginning with "Our policy is that ..." as in panel 22.

Panel 22

Our policy is that business hours run from 9:00 A.M. to 5:00 P.M.

The statement as worded assumes employees will do what is necessary to put it into practice. It is predicated on the good faith of the people it is directed to, and on its face it does not sound oppressive or confrontational.

Compared to the statement in panel 21, the wording in panel 19 sounds particularly dictatorial, almost combative. It's as if management expects that some people will not follow the rules, and words its policies to address that possibility proactively.

In general, simple declarative sentences make the best policy statements, as in the examples in panel 23.

Panel 23

A ten-minute grace period is offered for appointments.

Visitors are escorted while on the premises.

Individuals change their computer passwords at three month intervals.

Each statement is made as a present-day truth, a simple description of the way things look when they're done properly.

The Strictest Rules

Some individuals argue that this more respectful approach won't work in their organizations. They claim that compliance problems or their corporate culture forces them to be strict. They feel they have no choice but to start rules with phrases like "all employees must always," lest those employees think they aren't serious about the rule.

That claim confuses being strict with being dictatorial. We can learn a lesson about that difference from the world of criminal law, where rules are both strict and respectful.

I would venture to say that the strictest laws found in the world's English-speaking democracies are the **criminal** or **penal laws**. Assault on an individual, for example, is not tolerated in these jurisdictions, and they each have laws against it. Yet none is worded anything like the examples in panel 24.

Panel 24

All individuals must always refrain from assaulting anyone.

Assaulting others will not be tolerated.

People are strictly forbidden from assaulting one another. No exceptions will be made!

Laws aren't worded that way. In fact, a large majority of jurisdictions manage to draft absolute prohibitions on all kinds of activity without ever using the terms "must," "should," "never," and so on.

Instead, they use a series of simple, declarative statements set in the present tense. (A few jurisdictions use the future tense so they can sequence the declaration of criminality to occur after the action causing the problem.)

The *Texas Penal Code*, for example, prohibits assault using the language set out in panel 25.

Panel 25

"A person commits an offense if the person:

(1) intentionally, knowingly, or recklessly causes bodily injury to another ..."

Other jurisdictions split the statement into two parts: one part to define the term "assault" and one part to prohibit it. The New York State *Penal Code* starts off by explaining the different felony classes. Later, it defines what actions constitute assault.

When it comes to prohibiting those actions, the rule is written as shown in panel 26.

Panel 26

"Assault in the first degree is a class B felony."

It's simple and straight-forward, not dictatorial or aggressive.

Similarly, the *Criminal Code of Canada* wording is set out in panel 27.

Panel 27

"Every one who commits an assault is guilty of ...

(a) an indictable offence and is liable to imprisonment for a term not exceeding five years ..."

The New Zealand *Crimes Act* wording is set out in panel 28.

Panel 28

"Every one is liable to imprisonment for a term not exceeding 3 years who assaults any other person with intent ..."

The crimes prohibited by the various criminal codes vary from minor offences like spitting in public to the most major ones, such as murder, treason, and kidnapping. Yet they are all written in this same matter-of-fact tone of voice.

In other words, we have a situation where the strictest laws — for the most heinous crimes in the country — are written in more respectful language than the policies coming out of most organizations.

In fact, if you were to judge solely based on the tone of voice, you might be tempted to think that murdering your boss is not half as serious an offence as failing to replace the empty toner cartridge in the photocopier.

Clearly, the argument that strictness calls for dictatorially worded statements just doesn't hold water. The truth is that courtesy is simply unfamiliar to many as a rule-writing style.

It may take a little practice, but once you get the hang of it you'll find people respond much better than with the traditional marching-orders style.

Statements that Micro-Manage

Another way policy statements take on a parental tone is by micro-managing activities.

I'm sure you've seen many examples of overtly micro-managing statements, where the drafters are so concerned about the process that they list the individual steps required.

But often micro-management is more subtle than that. Look at the statement in panel 29.

Panel 29

Business areas must set aside time every year to review their equipment budgets for currency and accuracy.

Can you see the micro-management there?

The **result** we're looking for is some kind of annual feedback from the business areas. Presumably, we want that feedback to serve as input to a consolidated budget or forecast.

That being the case, the statement would be clearer if it **asked for that feedback** directly, along the lines of the statement in panel 30.

Panel 30

Business areas annually submit current and accurate equipment budgets.

Mandating that areas "set aside time" to do the work is gratuitous. Telling them to "review" the current budget before submitting a new one is plain old back-seat driving.

Writing a policy is not the same as writing a procedure. The point of a procedure is to walk the reader through a series of steps. Instructions like "set aside time for ..." and "review ..." are typical steps a procedure might include. It's not uncommon for a procedure to hold your hand while you work through it.

The same is not true for policy. If a business area were to submit a report, and you later learn that it hadn't formally set aside time for the review, would you hold that area in breach of policy? Obviously not. This rule is meant to achieve an outcome, not to quarterback the steps.

Part of the policy drafter's job is to separate the essential elements of a requirement from the non-essential ones. The essential elements belong in the policy because they establish lines you're not willing to cross. Supporting elements like "set aside time" and "review" are in fact just good advice, and advice belongs in the guidance documents.

Another example of micro-management is found in the statement in panel 31.

Panel 31

The Board of Directors formulates strategy at the broadest levels first and then moves to the development of more detailed strategies until the matter has been addressed to its satisfaction.

As well-intentioned as this statement might be, it doesn't belong in a policy document. It resembles a set of instructions. The tell-tale sign of the parental tone of voice is the clause "until the matter has been addressed to its satisfaction." (Kinda sounds like your mom telling you that you can't go out to play until you finish your homework, doesn't it?)

Panel 32 illustrates another example, one I come across all too often.

Panel 32

Employees must read, understand, and sign this policy.

This statement is another example of someone worrying about the steps rather than pursuing an objectively definable outcome. Do we actually expect to watch the employees reading the document? Not likely. Are we going to test employees on the contents to see how much of it was actually understood? Even less likely.

To word this statement correctly, it's important to pin down the result we really want. For most employers, that would be an indication from the employees of their willingness to be bound by the terms of the document.

Obviously, before committing themselves, competent individuals would read through the document first. If you then gave them the opportunity, they would ask questions about any parts they don't understand. It may be true that common sense isn't as common as we would like it to be, but a policy statement explicitly telling employees to "read and understand before signing" is blatantly treating them like children.

Without actually testing employees on the material, we won't really know their level of understanding of that document. Their own assessment of that level is of minimal value, because what they actually understand could be totally different from what we want them to understand.

What we really want from the employee in this situation is some **evidence of intent to comply** with the document. That evidence could be provided in a number of ways, from an oral acknowledgement to the employee's signature on a copy of the document.

A better wording of that statement is shown in panel 33.

Panel 33

Your signature at the bottom indicates your willingness to comply with the terms of this document.

Summary

When someone needs specific instructions to be able to complete a task, you can put those instructions in your guidance documents.

In an instructional document or a procedure, the individual steps provide clarity; in a policy they create clutter.

Chapter 7

BEING HELPFUL

Administrative and operational policies are meant to induce certain behaviours, with the expectation that the organization will be better able to do whatever it does.

In the past, the approach has been to induce behaviours by giving orders telling everyone what to do or, more typically, what not to do.

But today we know better. To get people's cooperation you need to engage them, not command them. There's no reason policy statements can't be positive, helping others do the right thing rather than threatening them against doing the wrong thing.

Turning Permissions into Invitations

Let's start with some simple cases.

Sometimes a "may" statement is really an invitation or an offer, but is worded as a permission. Look at the examples in panel 34.

Panel 34

Employees may eat lunch on the patio.

Employees may place small plants on their desks.

In these cases, the organization is doing something nice for the employees. But instead of wording it to be helpful, it has been worded to sound like a concession. The undertone is a subtext saying "we control this activity, but we're doing you a favour here. You may continue it as long as we continue to permit it."

Wouldn't it be nicer if it were worded graciously instead of dictatorially, as in panel 35?

Panel 35

Employees are invited to eat lunch on the patio.

Employees are welcome to place small plants on their desks.

Controlling Others

Often, an organization needs to impose a restriction of some sort on others. You can make a rule about the restriction — which will sound negative — or you can turn it into something positive and helpful.

As usual, we'll look at an obvious example before we transition to some subtler cases. Let's start with the policy statement in panel 36.

Panel 36

Other offices must not send us e-mail on the weekend.

You can see instantly that this statement is poorly worded. Obviously you can't control what workers in other offices do. Your policy owners lack the competence to govern people outside your own office.

But there's a more profound point to be made, what I call the Control Principle. We're making rules for adults here. The reality is that **you can't control what other people do; you can only control yourself. More specifically, you can only control how you respond to what others do.**

The policy statement around the timing of e-mail would be more sensible worded as in panel 37.

Panel 37

Our organization does not respond to e-mail messages on the weekend.

This wording makes it clear that we are controlling ourselves rather than others. You can send us messages all you like, but we won't look at them on the weekend.

The rule in panel 37 may be true as stated, but it sounds a little punitive. Instead of being appreciative that someone is providing us with information, it sounds like it's reproaching the sender for choosing timing that is inconvenient for us.

Modelled on the traditional rule format, it tells you what not to do and the consequences for disobeying.

A policy statement that sounds more appreciative and helpful would be worded as in panel 38.

Panel 38

E-mail messages received on the weekend will be answered Monday morning.

At the end of the day, our office routine is the same, but our attitude and approach to rule-writing have changed. We've gone from being prohibitory in panel 36 to being passively resistant in panel 37, and finally to being helpful in panel 38.

Theatre and symphony owners have understood this principle for a long time. They don't use the traditional rule format,

If you do x, then expect y.

On the event tickets, it doesn't say "If you arrive late, you will wait outside the door until we can seat you." Instead, the ticket says something like "Latecomers are seated at the first opportunity."

This wording is courteous and helpful. The unpleasant consequence of waiting at the back door is not being wielded as a punishment for disobedience; rather, it is being offered as the best experience they can provide given the circumstances.

Theatre owners can't control you, and they know it. They can only control how they respond to what you do, so their policy tells you what that response will be. As an adult, you can decide for yourself whether to be on time.

THE CONTROL PRINCIPLE

You can't control what other people do; you can only control how you respond to what they do.

Clarity of Response

The Control Principle has broad implications for all your policy statements. Employees are adults, and they will choose to follow — or ignore — rules based on their understanding of how you will respond to various circumstances.

Imagine an organization that wants employees to stop wearing shorts and sandals to work. It develops a policy with the statement found in panel 39.

Panel 39

Employees who deal with the public must dress appropriately.

The statement in panel 39 is typical of the requirements organizations write when trying to control employees' actions.

In its current form, the statement is a command.

(Side-note: Don't get distracted by the fact that this statement doesn't specify what "dressing appropriately" means. Yes, somewhere — in some standard or guidance document — "appropriate dress" may have to be described in more detail. The organization may even have done that already. Rules worded like the one in Panel 39 usually aren't a product of a lack of understanding of the details of the dress code, but more typically are a reaction to individuals who know what "dressing appropriately" means but are failing to do so.)

To make the statement more helpful, we need to understand what the organization will do if an employee does not follow this rule.

The organization can't control what individuals do and it can't control natural consequences. What it can control is its response to the situation. The statement in panel 40 sets out one possibility.

Panel 40

We send employees home for the day when they come to work dressed inappropriately.

That statement is a useful policy decision. The policy owner has determined specifically what the organization's actions will be in that situation. Expected behaviours are clear, and we know what will happen if the employee steps on the wrong side of the line.

The examples in panel 41 give us other possibilities.

Panel 41

We restrict employees who do not dress appropriately to back office duties.

We dock a day's pay from employees who do not dress appropriately.

When an employee comes to work dressed inappropriately, we make a notation in their file.

When compared to the examples above, it's clear that the "must" statement in panel 39 serves only to emphasize a master/servant relationship: "You will do this because we say you must. That reason is sufficient."

I find often, when a writer resorts to "must," that it's there **precisely because the organization has no clue about what it's going to do** when it encounters the problem.

That approach could be called "consequences by ambush." The organization hopes it can avoid making a decision about what the consequence will be until it's forced to; so, for the time being, it circumscribes the issue by using "must." This approach is effectively an avoidance technique. (It reminds me of my grandmother, who would say, "you'd better listen to me and not push me, because you don't know what I'm going to do when I'm pushed!")

This is not to suggest that every policy statement has to include consequences. The statement in panel 42 represents a valid decision despite the lack of overt consequences in the sentence.

42

> The company considers delivery personnel to be ready and able to work when they
>
> + arrive no later than 8 o'clock in the morning
> + are not under the influence of any intoxicating substance or medication, and
> + are in possession of their driver's licence.

This statement in panel 42 works because it draws the line between left and right. To complete the picture, we will need a statement around the implications of not being "ready and able to work" somewhere else in our documentation.

Summary

If you take only one thing from reading this book, I hope it's the Control Principle: you can't control what other people do; you can only control how you respond to what they do.

Chapter 8

MUST, MAY, AND SHOULD

Despite their pervasiveness in policy instruments, these terms are antiquated. They have two serious shortcomings: (1) they are **heavy-handed** and (2) they **lack clarity**.

1. Heavy-Handedness

"Must," "may," and "should" are all born of a Parent–Child[1] dynamic. They all convey an undertone saying, "Remember that we are in charge."

"Must" is a mandate. "You will do this because we say so."

"May" is a dispensation. "We, in our benevolence, grant you permission to do this."

"Should" is a concession. "Even though we could make this mandatory, we're content merely to recommend it."

All three of the terms reinforce an underlying presumption that two diverse sets of interests are involved: rule makers and rule followers. That presumption alone is divisive and a barrier to a collaborative work environment.

---

[1] These terms come from the science of Transactional Analysis. For a simple explanation of the Parent–Child and Adult–Adult dynamics, see *Games People Play*, by Eric Berne, M.D.

Take the example in panel 43.

Panel 43

Employees must not park in the fire lane behind the building.

That statement unnecessarily segments the workforce. The truth is that **no one** is permitted to park in the fire lane outside of emergency vehicles, management included.

Wording the rule differently captures the strictness without being divisive, as shown in panel 44.

Panel 44

Vehicles parked in the fire lane behind the building will be towed.

Now it's clear that the rule applies to everybody.

To reflect an attitude more appropriate for the modern workplace, we want to move our rules away from implying a Parent–Child dynamic in favour of an Adult–Adult dynamic, wherever possible.

2. Lack of Clarity

No doubt, in some corners old habits die hard. Those three modal verbs have become fossilized in policy language, and some writers fear dropping them on the grounds that doing so would sacrifice clarity.

In reality, all three verbs are ambiguous in far too many contexts. We'll look at each modal verb in turn to see the various discrete meanings each one conveys.

The Conventional Approach

The conventional approach to indicating the relative strictness of these three words can be summarized as follows:

+ "Must" means mandatory.
+ "May" means permitted.
+ "Should" means recommended.

The International Standards Organization (ISO) uses a similar model. According to ISO,

+ "'Shall' indicates a requirement.
+ 'Should' indicates a recommendation.
+ 'May' is used to indicate that something is permitted.
+ 'Can' is used to indicate that something is possible."[2]

These definitions are problematic from the get-go.

No Distinction in the Negative

When the terms "must" and "may" appear in the negative, the mandatory/optional distinction between them all but disappears completely.

Compare the A and B statements in panel 45.

---

[2] "Expressions in ISO International Standards And Other Normative ISO Deliverables." https://www.iso.org/foreword-supplementary-information.html

---

Panel 45

A) Documents may not be removed from the office.

B) Documents must not be removed from the office.

At the end of the day, these two statements produce identical results. Granted, technically in the first case an action is "not permitted" and in the second it is "forbidden," but in neither case are you allowed to remove documents from the office.

You might argue that using "may" puts the restriction more politely, and I suppose that's a possibility. Nonetheless, in this context **"may" doesn't offer an option.** The requirement is simply more politely mandatory.

In negative statements, therefore, the argument that the modal verbs preserve a mandatory/optional distinction is untenable. So let's put aside the negative forms and simply look at positive statements. Is the argument any stronger?

The Ambiguities of "Must"

In traditional policy wording, writers use "must" to indicate a mandatory requirement, as in panel 46.

Panel 46

When the fire alarm rings, everyone must exit the building.

The word "must" in this statement imposes an obligation. We can confirm that interpretation by testing how the sentence reads when the notion of obligation is made explicit, as in panel 47.

Panel 47

When the fire alarm rings, everyone is obligated to exit the building.

That is the plain and simple meaning of "must." And if "must" always expanded to "is obligated to," we'd have no problem. But the word "must" is used in several other ways. Besides creating an obligation, policy writers use it to

+ grant an authority,
+ set a condition of eligibility, or
+ declare an entitlement.

Look at the typical example set out in panel 48.

Panel 48

The vice-president must approve all requests to borrow company equipment.

The owner of the policy wasn't intending to **obligate** the vice-president to grant these requests, but that's the way the statement reads. The drafter tried to make something mandatory, and used the word "must" to do that. In fact, that "must" is misplaced, so we have to dig around to figure out exactly what the mandatory element is supposed to be.

One interpretation of the original intention is that an approval is required to borrow equipment and **that approval must come from the vice-president.**

If that's what was intended to be conveyed, then the policy decision is about **authority.** The intent of the rule is to give the vice-president the sole authority to approve the request. It has nothing whatsoever to do with obligation.

If we articulated that rule clearly instead of merely implying it, we would end up with the statement in panel 49.

Panel 49

The vice-president has the authority to approve requests to borrow company equipment.

The intent is now clear: we're not requiring anybody to do anything; we're simply granting an authority to an individual who can choose when to exercise it. There's no "must" about it.

Note how this new wording manages to retain the **strictness of the original rule,** but **completely eliminates the need to distinguish between mandatory and optional actions.**

An alternate interpretation of the example in panel 48 is that it mandates the order of events in a process. The intent is to make the vice-president's approval a pre-condition to borrowing the equipment. In that case, the decision is again not about obligation at all, but about **eligibility.** The intent is to make equipment ineligible to be borrowed until after the vice-president's approval has been given.

So let's say that more clearly, as in panel 50.

Panel 50

Company equipment can be loaned out upon the approval of the vice-president.

With this rewording, just like the previous one, we're being helpful, offering to open a door, rather than being restrictive and throwing down an impediment.

Sometimes, management is so intent on using "must" in the rules that it gets inserted even when it makes no sense at all. Look at the example in panel 51.

Panel 51

Employees must be given access to their own personnel files upon request.

If the "must" here is supposed to obligate someone to do something, it's not clear who that someone is. Again, we have to dig deep to figure out what's going on.

The intention obviously wasn't to obligate employees to look at their files. If anyone is being mandated to take action here, it would be someone who can provide access to the files. The "must" was meant to obligate that individual

— who isn't even mentioned — to produce the files upon the employees' request.

The intent here is not to establish obligation; rather, it is about **entitlement**. Employees who wish to see their files are entitled to see them. So we should say just that, as in panel 52.

Panel 52

Employees are entitled to have access to their own personnel files.

Early on in this book I noted that most people want to do the right thing. I'd rather proceed on the assumption that when someone who is entitled to see a file asks for it, the individuals controlling file access will be happy to oblige. We don't need to order them to comply.

Summary of "Must"

No one likes being commanded to do something. A mandatory requirement can be reworded to avoid both the ambiguity and the condescending overtones of the word "must" by declaring the authority, eligibility, or entitlement directly.

Simply by dropping the word "must" in these situations, we are no longer dividing the office into rule makers and rule followers, no longer barking orders, and we avoid the Parent–Child dynamic.

The Ambiguities of "May"

In traditional policy wording, writers use "may" to indicate that someone is being given an option. But like "must," that word suffers from misplacement and misuse in two ways.

First, mandatory requirements are often hidden inside "may" statements. In these cases no real options are available, but the drafters want to avoid the word "must" to soften the blow.

Take the example in panel 53.

Panel 53

Private storage devices may be used on corporate computers only with the approval of the IT branch.

The drafters would argue that they chose "may be used" instead of "must be used" because they're not trying to force anyone to use the devices. In this case, they would argue, "may" indicates that at least one option is being offered.

But don't be fooled: there are more "musts" than options in that statement. If you want to use a private storage device on a corporate computer, the policy dictates that

+ you **must** obtain approval,
+ that approval **must** come from the IT Branch, and
+ you **must** refrain from using the device until you get that approval.

The **only** optional part of the situation is your decision to want to use a device in the first place.

The statement in panel 53 is a set of mandatory requirements masquerading as an optional one. A more honest wording would state that overtly, for example, using the wording in panel 54.

Panel 54

Approval from the IT branch is required before connecting any private storage devices.

Second, just like "must," "may" often entails ambiguity around exactly which element it governs.

Consider the statement in panel 55.

Panel 55

Employees may discuss flexible hours with their supervisors.

Again, the drafters of the statement would argue that they used "may" instead of "must" because they're not trying to force a discussion, but rather to provide the option. The problem here is that "may" is permitting the wrong action. That problem becomes obvious when we test the sentence in its negative form, as in panel 56.

Panel 56

Employees may not discuss flexible hours with their supervisors.

What exactly is meant to be prohibited in panel 56 but permitted in panel 55? Is it the flexible hours themselves or the discussions about them?

If the original intent is to permit the use of flexible hours, that could be stated a lot more clearly, as in panel 57.

Panel 57

Employees have the option to work flexible hours.

If the intent is to permit the discussions about them ... well, we've just turned the clock back 50 years. Do we really need a formal policy statement to permit two individuals to discuss something?

The statement in panel 55 is not easily fixed because it implies a lot of conditions but doesn't actually state anything specific. It implies that flexible hours might be allowed and it implies that the supervisor has some role in that process, but beyond that it doesn't tell us much. We can't know when we are or are not in compliance with this statement.

Other Words of Permission

Whenever "may" is used to grant permission, it creates a Parent–Child dynamic. Other words granting permission do the same, including terms like the following:

+ are permitted
+ are acceptable
+ are allowed
+ are authorized.

To this list we can add the negative form of each, such as "are not permitted" and "are disallowed," as well as a few other heavy-handed terms:

+ are not tolerated
+ are banned
+ are off limits
+ are prohibited
+ are (strictly) forbidden.

Summary of "May"

Virtually all uses of the word "may" are instances purporting to provide options in a situation. In fact, the options they offer are typically obvious once we know the conditions and restrictions. We can avoid both the ambiguity and the patronizing overtones of the word "may" simply by specifying the conditions or restrictions. By doing that, we are no longer granting permissions, and again, we have avoided the Parent–Child dynamic.

The Ambiguities of "Should"

Of the three modal verbs discussed here, "should" suffers the worst identity crisis. It is the most versatile of the terms, and with that, the most ambiguous.

Policy drafters reach for "should" to convey a recommendation, in contrast to a mandatory requirement. An example is shown in panel 58.

Panel 58

Employees should change their passwords every 90 days.

Since it's only a recommendation, it can be recast as in panel 59.

Panel 59

It is strongly recommended that employees change their passwords every 90 days.

A recommendation statement is meaningless in a rule-based context. Since the action is not mandatory, an employee cannot be disciplined for not following it.

One of our goals in creating rules is to draw a line in the sand clearly letting others know when they are on- or off-side. But we can't be off-side with a "should" statement. Actions that are merely recommended are technically "optional." But you won't see the word "optional" too often in a policy. Drafters tend to avoid that word thinking it sounds weak.

The truth is, in this case, the password-changing recommendation itself is weak. At its strongest, the statement is an insipid plea to do the right thing without making it a rule; at its weakest, it's a declaration of a best practice.

You will recall that the documentation framework places authorities in one column and guidance in another. These recommendations are not decisions. They belong in your guidance documents, office manuals, and wall posters.

A well-written authority expressly mandates a practice, permits it, or prohibits it. What it doesn't do is sit on the fence.

The Many Meanings of "Should"

Setting the policy/advice distinction aside, we still have the precise meaning of "should" to resolve.

Masking Mandatory Statements

Take, for example, the typical statement shown in panel 60.

Panel 60

The fire exit should be used only in emergencies.

Is that really intended as a recommendation rather than a mandatory rule? If the organization has no intention of enforcing it, then the statement is really no more than advice.

More likely, this statement was meant to be a strict rule, and "should" was used as a muted or blunted "must." Writers reach for a blunted must when they have to make a strict rule but don't want it to sound strict — which actually defeats the purpose, doesn't it?

Other examples are found in panel 61.

Panel 61

Passengers should pay their fare upon boarding the bus.

Employees should report all on-site injuries within 48 hours.

The application should be signed and dated at the bottom.

In none of those examples is "should" intended to be a mere recommendation.

As you might expect, using "should" in this sense in policy documents is a recipe for disaster. Someone will inevitably insist that this "should" statement **is** a mere recommendation, arguing that if the action were intended as a firm rule it would have been made mandatory.

Ethical Obligations

Another common use of "should" is to indicate a moral or ethical obligation. Take the statements in panel 62.

Panel 62

Service representatives should strive to treat complaints with compassion.

Informational brochures should avoid racial and sexual stereotyping.

In negotiations around a pre-nuptial agreement, lawyers should not represent both parties.

Although they use the word "should," these statements are intended to be **stronger than recommendations but not as strong as mandatory requirements**. The use of "should" in these cases suggests the driver behind the rule is some moral or ethical principle.

Codes of conduct and ethical codes — discussed more fully in Chapter 10 — often use "should" to modify verbs, but the possibility for ambiguity is just as real in those documents. The sentence in panel 63 is typical.

Panel 63

Employees should avoid conflicts of interest.

Which of the following meanings — listed in descending order of degrees of strictness — is the "should" in panel 63 supposed to convey?

+ Always avoid them.
+ Avoid them whenever possible.
+ Try to avoid them.

+ Avoid them unless you have a good reason not to.

+ Avoid them unless you have any reason not to.

+ Avoid them if you want to stay out of the news.

Actually, we can't know which degree is intended without speaking to the person who drafted the statement.

Some drafters justify "should" in these situations precisely because they want to rely on that ambiguity. They expect that ambiguity to enable flexibility in interpretation. To my mind, that flexibility reflects a lack of clarity. If you really want flexibility, then say that, as in panel 64.

Panel 64

When determining whether a conflict of interest exists, each situation is assessed on its own merits.

Other Uses of "Should"

The word "should" is a master of disguises. Look at the examples in panel 65.

Panel 65

Information should be accessible, current, and accurate.

Skills training should be available to all employees.

We ship orders within 48 hours. Customers should receive them no later than seven days after that.

Welcome to the office! Inside your desk drawer you should find a laptop computer and a key.

Although they use the word "should," these statements are neither recommendations, nor softened mandatory requirements, nor ethical imperatives.

In these cases, "should" conveys a target, a probability, or an **expectation**. Whichever it is, they all make for weak policy statements. In each case, it's not clear what action you can take to be compliant.

Other uses of "should" are shown in panels 66, 67, and 68.

Panel 66

Should more information be required, the application form will be returned.

Should the item not be available, the customer's money will be refunded.

In panel 66, "should" expresses a **possibility** or **eventuality**, almost acting like a synonym for the word "if."

Panel 67

I should have said something to her at the time.

In panel 67, "should" indicates an expression of **regret** or **reassessment**.

Panel 68

I should think you would know that by now.

In panel 68, "should" is a formal alternative to the conditional modal "would."

Summary of "Should"

In addition to conveying a recommendation, the word "should" can indicate any of the following:

+ good advice
+ a requirement
+ a target or governing principle
+ a probability or expectation
+ a possibility or eventuality
+ regret
+ conditional tense

When "should" indicates a mandatory requirement, it is being misused. In all other cases it is potentially ambiguous.

Fortunately, all the "should" statements covered in this section are appropriate for a guidance document, where you can add more words to provide helpful context.

You might decide, after reading this section, that you still want your policy to contain statements of recommendation. In that case, to reduce the possibility for confusion, limit the use of "should" to **genuine recommendations** and eliminate all other instances.

Conclusion

It would be incongruous, for obvious reasons, if I said, "you must never use 'must,' or you should never use 'should.'" So I won't say that.

Most policy decisions can be written without resorting to the modal verbs "must," "may," or "should." My practice is to think through what the decision is really about, so I avoid the tension between "mandatory" and "optional" completely.

To be candid, I'd be lying if I claimed that I **never** use these modal verbs. They are certainly convenient. We're so used to them, it's almost formulaic to include them.

It's also easy to slip them into a draft policy being submitted for approval without anyone objecting. So many policy-makers are used to rules written in that tone of voice that they don't register the implications until it's too late.

My practice today is to review all my writing to check my use of "must," "may," and "should." Where I am able to reword the sentence without using the modal verb, I do that. If I can't avoid the modal, then I make sure the sentence is as clear as possible.

Chapter 9

STANDARDS

My neighbour Susan starts all her recipes with two medium onions and a clove of garlic sautéed in olive oil and white wine. That's her standard cooking base. If we wrote that down and named it the "Standard Onion Base," then any time we want to use it in a recipe we can say simply, "Start with the standard onion base, then add ...."

In Chapter 4 we looked at a number of policy instrument titles, and I suggested that you set aside the title "standard" because it was different from the others.

A **standard** is a set of specifications. The specifications can be technical or mundane — from the most precise scientific measurement, like "5.65425 grams," to the most general of descriptions, like "between half-full and full."

A standard wraps one or more specifications into a set, so they can be referred to as a unit. It acts as a shortcut to save us from repeatedly writing out sets of specifications every time we need them.

Mandatory or Optional?

One of the policy-making committees I sat on used to argue endlessly among themselves over the statements going into their standards. Some members of the committee wanted the rule to offer the choice between standard A and standard B, and to call these standards "optional." Others insisted that anything called a "standard" has to be mandatory, and they couldn't wrap their heads around how something could be mandatory and optional at the same time.

The result was that all the decisions produced by this committee were very, very rigid. Each specification in every standard was mandatory; they left no room for themselves to manoeuvre through difficult areas.

This group was confused about the role of a standard inside a policy suite. The confusion arises from failing to distinguish the **level of rigour around the specifications** inside the standard from the **level of rigour around the organization's adoption** of the standard.

A standard can be adopted as mandatory or optional. When an organization mandates a standard, its use becomes compulsory. When an organization recommends the standard, its use is merely optional. But being optional doesn't render it any less of a standard.

An illustration might help clarify the distinction.

Office Paper

In North America, paper for printers and photocopiers can be purchased in a number of standard sizes, the most common of which are letter, legal, and tabloid. Each of these standards has a prescribed height and a prescribed width. In the rest of the world, the most common standards are A3, A4, and A5, and similarly each of these has a prescribed height and a prescribed width.

The specifications in each standard are mandatory. There is no flexibility here. You can't alter dimensions of the paper without offending the standard.

Each organization decides which of these paper sizes it will use. It might decide to rely solely on A3, A4, and A5, or it might decide to mix standards and use A4, legal, and tabloid.

The organization's policy decisions declare whether each standard is mandatory, optional, or disallowed.

Calibre of a Standard

A standard is only as good as its certifying body.

The American National Standards Institute (ANSI) offers a standard containing technical specifications around the types and classes of protective industrial helmets — commonly known as "hard hats." This standard is backed by the stellar reputation that ANSI has managed to build for itself over the years.

Let's say that Marie and Paul run a family construction business in a small town in the Midwest. Their business decides to establish its own standard for helmets. They write out the technical specifications they think are appropriate, and title the document Marie and Paul's Helmet Standards.

Which standard would you rather adopt? My bet is that Marie and Paul don't have a lot of credibility in your eyes. Where you have a choice, you choose your standard according to your needs.

True, in areas like safety and security, the government may already have taken the reins and mandated the use of specific standards, so you may not have much of a choice. In many areas, however, you have complete choice of which standard you wish to adopt.

Building a Standard

You can create your own standards simply by assembling a set of desired specifications and packaging them in a document. A sample standard, calling itself Standard #21 and setting out the specifications around office correspondence, is found in Figure 6.

Standard #21, now written out for certainty and signed by the experts who created it, can be incorporated by reference into your other policy instruments.

Drafting Respectful Standards

This heading is a trick!

A standard itself is neither respectful nor disrespectful. A standard is neutral. It is simply a list of specifications.

A well-written standard does not contain the words "must," "must not," "should," or other terms of obligation. It doesn't contain instructions, or commands, or suggestions. The only things it contains are specifications, and no one needs to take those personally.

Adopting a Standard

An organization adopts a standard by making a policy decision, along the lines of those offered in panel 69.

FIGURE 6—STANDARD FOR OFFICE CORRESPONDENCE

Standard #21
Office Correspondence

Font
Arial 12 pt. Roman

Date Position
Top left

Date Format
YYYY-MM-DD

RE: line
Boldface, no underline

Closing
Yours, sincerely

Panel 69

Paper size A4 is used for documents.

Correspondence is printed on Letter size paper.

Budget spreadsheets are formatted for printing on Tabloid size paper.

Documents produced conform to Standard #21 — Office Correspondence.

Mandatory Adoption

Statements like those in panel 69 are sufficient to establish the mandatory adoption of a given standard. If deviation from the standard is a real concern, the wording can be strengthened, as in panel 70.

Panel 70

For correspondence, the organization uses paper size A4 exclusively.

Optional Adoption

An organization may choose to permit but not mandate a given standard. Two examples of statements adopting an optional standard are found in panel 71.

Panel 71

In advertising materials, measurements are expressed in metric units alone or in combination with Imperial units.

In advertising materials, measurements are expressed in U.S. standard units, metric units, or both.

In the first statement in panel 71, the metric standard is mandatory and the Imperial standard is optional.

In the second statement both standards are permitted and the use of at least one is mandatory.

Prohibition

In the face of a statement that standard A has been adopted, an inference that standard B is disallowed can be made. But if necessary, a statement can explicitly indicate when a standard is not to be used, as in panel 72.

Panel 72

Tabloid size paper is not used in the office.

Correspondence is printed on A4 size paper. The use of Letter size paper is discontinued.

Note that the statements in panel 72 do not use loaded words like "disallowed" or "prohibited." Those kinds of words are essentially expressions of a power dynamic of the dominant over the behaviours of the subordinate. The policy is written respectfully when it describes the state of affairs of the organization's activities without re-emphasizing the power structure.

Enacting a Standard

For the standard to have authority, it needs to be enacted. It cannot enact itself; that enactment needs to come from somewhere else.

In the year 1859 a resident of San Francisco, California, proclaimed himself "Emperor of the United States."[3]

Born Joshua Abraham Norton in England, he is estimated to have arrived in San Francisco sometime in 1849. His imperial decrees, all intended to improve the nation, included abolishing the U.S. Congress and sending the army in to clear out the government buildings in Washington, D.C. In addition, he commanded the Roman Catholic and Protestant churches to recognize his sovereignty, ordered the Republican and Democratic parties to disband, and — in what was obviously a rare lucid moment — banned the use of the moniker "Frisco" for the city.

Stories from that time tell of the occasional deference granted by locals to the man and his eccentricities. Oddly, though, all the official organizations targeted in his edicts completely ignored him. Maybe he was missing some of the paperwork necessary to validate claims of imperial authority. Who knew they were so sticky about those things back then?

The lesson of this story is simple: self-declaration of one's own power is insufficient to support a claim of authority.

---

3 https://en.wikipedia.org/wiki/Emperor_Norton

Sadly, the position of Emperor of the United States remains formally vacant even today.

Legitimacy comes from without, not from within. A person can claim any authority or entitlement in the world; however, to be valid, something external to that person needs to support the claim.

A standard that declares itself mandatory is not unlike Mr. Norton. Citing an authority inside the standard doesn't make a difference: even if Mr. Norton had held the position of Emperor based on an Act of Congress, when it comes to the paperwork most of us would want to see that Act where the appointment is spelled out rather than merely trusting Mr. Norton's self-serving assurances.

When a foreign ambassador shows up on your doorstep asking to be accorded the rights of a resident diplomat, you are unlikely to grant that status to her in the absence of some evidence of the appointment. That evidence would need at least to look like it was issued by the foreign government. A self-serving note scrawled by the diplomat isn't going to cut it.

The same principle applies in the policy world. **A standard declaring itself to be mandatory is in fact making a self-serving statement.** It's not a legitimate way of indicating authenticity.

The best approach to implementing a standard is to have two elements:

- ✦ the standard itself, containing the required technical specifications, and
- ✦ a policy instrument containing an **enacting statement**.

The enacting statement mandates, recommends, or permits the standard.

This bipartite approach has two benefits. First, the use of separate documents gives an organization complete flexibility to mandate different levels of applicability to different situations and organizational units. Policy instruments can contain statements such as those found in panel 73.

Panel 73

Web pages published by group A conform to Standards #10 and #12.

Web pages published by group B conform to Standards #10, #11, and #14.

Web pages published by group C need not conform to any standard.

In this way, **a standard can be simultaneously mandated, permitted, recommended, and disallowed in different circumstances.** Even if that flexibility doesn't seem necessary at the moment, it may become useful in the future.

The second benefit is that this separation more accurately reflects the two distinct areas of accountability involved. Crafting a standard involves a different set of decisions from crafting the policy enacting it.

Those who shape the specifications in a standard are subject matter experts. They thereby become the owners of the standard, and they are accountable for ensuring that each specification is technically defensible. **Fixing a technical specification is a technical decision**, not a management one.

In contrast, **enacting the standard is a management decision**, not a technical one. By embedding the enacting statement inside a policy, the policy owners take responsibility for the decision around its adoption.

Let's look at how that split works in practice. Assume a business is operating a chain of restaurants. The food safety experts have put together a cleaning standard, shown in panel 74, to be used when closing down at the end of each day.

Panel 74

Kitchen Shut-Down Standard

+ Surfaces scrubbed with antiseptic cleaning solution.
+ Refrigerators set to 4°C / 40°F.
+ Heating surfaces cooled to room temperature and set to Off.
+ Perishables double-wrapped in plastic, then stored in plastic, glass, or metal containers.

After reviewing this standard, senior management agrees to make it mandatory for every restaurant in the chain.

What if someone in the organization were to object? Separating the owner of the standard from the owner of the policy helps us direct the objection up the right ladder.

Victor, for example, thinks double-wrapping food before putting it into a container is overkill. He argues that double-wrapping doesn't keep the rolls any fresher than single wrapping. Victor can first take his objection up with the owner of the standard. As subject matter experts, owners of standards are in a position to entertain technical discussions.

Sophia objects for a different reason: she claims that implementing the standard would cost too much time and money and will dig into the profits. That objection can be raised with the policy owner, because it is the owner who decides whether a standard is mandatory, optional, or recommended. When weighing the merits of Sophia's objection, the policy owner may seek out the standard owner to hear its side of the argument. At the end of the day, though, it's the policy owner who decides whether the hardship imposed on the business is more or less important than the technical consequences foreseen by the subject matter experts.

Summary

Separating the policy statements from the standards permits the allocation of accountability for the decisions to the appropriate places in the organization.

Chapter 10

CODES OF CONDUCT

We are witnessing an increase in public awareness of the need to establish value statements around politically "hot" issues, such as racial and gender diversity, sexual harassment, and systemic bias. This increased awareness has bred a recognition that organizations lose credibility when they operate in ignorance of the world's injustices. Organizations are being called on to relinquish their positions of silence and demonstrate their commitments visibly by taking an active or pro-active stand on issues. As a result, codes of conduct have recently become a priority.

A code of conduct is a special type of authority. It records the collective commitment of those who adopt it — specifically, a commitment to pursue a set of common values.

Stylistically, a code of conduct has more in common with an organization's vision statement or a declaration of principles than with the typical compilation of specific rules that becomes a policy or directive. It may validly set targets without an indication of how to reach them, because the targets are worthy in and of themselves.

Tone of Voice Still Matters

If using the wrong tone of voice in policies and directives results in a lack of employee engagement, the effect is doubly pronounced in a code of conduct. When comprised of a series of statements giving you instructions on how to be a good person, the code loses credibility around the moral authority it purports to espouse.

Panel 75 shows a few sentences extracted from a real code of conduct that I came across in my travels. (Grammar errors and the use of boldface are preserved.)

Panel 75

To make clear what is expected, everyone is **required to conform** to the following Code of Conduct. [Management] will enforce this code.

We assume that most people are intelligent and well-intended. However, we've recently come to see that sometimes it's necessary to spell out the behavior we support and don't support.

The core of our approach is this: we will do whatever we believe is necessary to ensure that our organization is a safe and productive environment for everyone.

Don't harass people. We do not tolerate harassment of other employees in any form.

Or else. Employees violating these rules will be asked to leave the organization.

You get the picture.

Clearly, this document speaks in a tone of voice entirely antithetical to what management wants to achieve. The language is divisive, intending to distinguish those making the rules from others who are supposed to follow them. There is no attempt to engage or build the communal rapport so critical to the success of a code of conduct.

When I first read this document, I felt attacked. It was as if the organization pushing it didn't trust me to be a decent person, or even to know what being a decent person means. The entire approach is confrontational. I'm in no way appeased by the half-hearted compliment at the beginning of the second paragraph, because it feels like false flattery.

The sentence that screams the management attitude of this document is in the middle, saying "we will do whatever we believe is necessary." In one eight-word clause, management dismisses your contribution to the success of this initiative as secondary to its intent to control the situation.

The fourth paragraph is the ultimate definition of irony: a strong reprimand telling you that strong reprimands are not tolerated. The fifth paragraph is entirely devoted to issuing a threat.

We can do better than this. If *any* policy document deserves to be written in a positive, courteous, and respectful manner, it would be a code of conduct that says we are positive, courteous, and respectful.

"We" Statements

The whole point of a code of conduct is to be a guide we can all buy into. The targets are set for individuals to support the collective. There is nothing being asked of the reader that doesn't apply equally to the writer.

The most impactful style for codes of conduct, value statements, and declarations of principles are sentences written in the first person plural, as in panel 76.

Panel 76

+ We value trust, candour, and professionalism.
+ We believe all people are worthy of our respect.
+ We strive to give every customer our full attention.
+ We actively promote the organization's values in every interaction with the public and with other employees.
+ We disclose all potential conflicts of interest as soon as we become aware of them.

And so on.

Statements written in the simple present tense are far more impactful than those written in the imperative. They embody the true spirit of a code of conduct, acting as a rallying cry rather than a set of marching orders handed down from headquarters. It's no accident that the U.S. Declaration of Independence uses the same approach: "We hold these truths to be self-evident...."

Panel 77 provides examples of statements for use in a code of conduct that are consistent with the values it espouses.

Panel 77

We are sensitive to the needs of others around us, use good judgment, and treat others with respect.

We comply immediately with direct requests to stop a behaviour that is considered harassment. Specifically, we do not initiate or engage in the following:

+ Offensive verbal comments or jokes related to gender, sexual orientation, disability, language, physical appearance, body size, race, or religion
+ Presentation of sexual images
+ Intimidation, stalking, or unwanted following
+ Sustained disruption to proceedings
+ Inappropriate or unwelcome physical contact or sexual attention
+ Public shaming

When we are asked to leave the space of an incident based on an alleged infraction of this code, we do so immediately, quietly, and without drawing attention to the situation.

You can see how these positively worded statements are much more inclusive, more respectful, and more in keeping with the intent of a code of conduct.

Tough Situations

Just to be clear, I recognize that sometimes you have more pits than cherries. There are times when situations have become intolerable and your organization needs to lower the hammer. In those cases, you may need written statements in an authority that provide security should you wish to take measures to deal with conflict, even if you reach for them as a last resort.

But the place to spell out those measures is not the code of conduct. If you have heavy artillery, put it in some other policy. A well-written code of conduct doesn't need to warn you that it's prepared to do battle.

As a Foundational Document

A participant in one of my workshops stood up to tell the group that her organization believes its Code of Conduct to be the foundation of its policy suite. Having a strong code of conduct to fall back on meant that her organization could do without many rules that other organizations are forced to put into policies. The guidance was informed by statements in the Code about acting honestly, professionally, equitably … and so on.

That approach wouldn't work for many organizations, but it will for some. It's an intriguing approach, worthy of some exploration.

Ethical Codes

An ethical code is not the same as a code of conduct, and the rules for drafting one differ slightly.

In an ethical code, the justification compelling a course of action is an ethical duty. Take the example in panel 78.

Panel 78

Board members have an ethical duty to disclose any potential conflicts of interest.

The drafter makes a stylistic decision at the beginning: will the four-word phrase "has an ethical duty" appear throughout the document, or will it be shortened to "must" or "should" or something similar, as in panel 79?

Panel 79

Board members must disclose any potential conflicts of interest.

In these cases, where it is made clear that "must" is to be interpreted as "has an ethical duty," the undertones of that word discussed in earlier chapters are less pronounced. This "must" is not born of a Parent–Child relationship; rather, it reflects how serious the approval body is about using ethical concerns to drive duties.

Some drafters prefer to use "should" in these cases, as in panel 80.

Panel 80

Board members should disclose any potential conflicts of interest.

In these cases, "should" means "has an ethical duty," and it emphasizes that the duty is ethical rather than legal. The same advice around making the interpretation clear applies here.

My only caution is that consistency is critical. There's nothing wrong with using "must" or "should" in a code of ethics to stand in for "has an ethical duty," so long as all instances of "must" or "should" in the document have that meaning, rather than one of the many alternate meanings described in Chapter 8.

Summary

A code of conduct is an appeal to unite under a common set of values. It doesn't inspire much confidence when those values include respect and courtesy but you can't see them in the writing style.

Chapter 11

PACKAGING

While **policy statements form the core** of your policy instruments, they still need to be packaged properly. When the information preceding and following the core of the document is standardized for your organization, it makes the policy suite easier to navigate.

Packaging involves a series of components, each discussed in detail in this chapter.

Examples are found in the sample *Clean Desk Policy* at the end of the book.

1. Title

The policy instrument begins with a title. Short and sweet is the way to go.

I recommend that the instrument type appear as the first word, thereby avoiding confusing titles such as "Writing Policy" and "New Service Standard" when you really mean "Policy on Writing" and "Standard on New Service."

Enough said.

2. Policy Owner

The identity of the policy owner is the first piece of information to appear below the title. The legitimacy of every statement after that point is predicated on that owner having the competence to make those decisions.

Even when all the policies in an organization have the same owner, it is still good practice to list that owner at the top of each policy. At some point in the future, the owner — be that an individual, a committee, or a delegated entity — might change, and you will want to be able to identify with certainty whether the policy instrument was approved by the new or the old entity.

3. Dates

Critical Dates

Two critical dates appear near the top of the policy.

Approval date

The first is the date of approval of the policy instrument by the owner.

The appearance of this date on the document is a record-keeping requirement. To the degree that the policy document acts as an official record of the decisions in it, the approval date is a key piece of data for evidentiary purposes. Together, the identity of the owner and the date of approval are the policy equivalent of signing and dating a piece of correspondence.

Due-for-Review Date

The second is the date the policy instrument is due for review.

This due-for-review date is the equivalent of the "best before" date found on a jar of pickles. The pickles may be safe after that date, but you know to inspect the jar a little more carefully.

A due-for-review date is better than an expiry date, because it doesn't leave you without a valid policy if you don't renew it in time. The policy will still be in force and users will be alert to exercise caution.

Once the policy has been reviewed, if no changes are required to the text, then the only change to the document is to set a new due-for-review date.

Other Dates

Last Modified Date

The date the policy was **last modified** is an important piece of document management information, as it is with many types of documents. The version number, version date, or last modified date can appear in the same place you put it in all your other documents; or, you may choose to suppress it on the final versions.

I personally like the version number to appear at all times, and I find that the easiest way to manage versions is

+ to use the last modified date as the version number — for example, version 2020-08-24, and
+ to place that version number in a document footer appearing on each page.

Effective Date

The date the policy becomes **effective** is not part of the packaging. It is as important a decision by the owner as any other statement in the policy. For that reason, it **appears in the core of the document**.

By convention, in legal documents the effective date normally appears as **either the first or the last statement** in the core.

4. Policy Objective

A simple opening statement crisply sets out the objective of the policy.

Lengthy preambles do not belong in the policy instrument. The old practice of beginning a policy with series of "Whereas" paragraphs announces to the world that you have not kept up with the times.

The policy objective needs to be easily recited when explaining the policy. The shorter and simpler the objective, the easier it is to convey.

Distinguish the policy objective, which belongs in the policy, from background information, which does not. If it's necessary to provide background information to the reader, you can put that information into a companion document to the policy or in the guidance. Almost invariably, background information stale-dates long before the policy itself.

Policy Objective Versus Subject Objective

This is a fine but important distinction.

The policy objective is a statement about **why you are producing the policy instrument**, not why the subject of the policy instrument is important.

The objective is what the policy instrument achieves, not what policy compliance achieves.

Panel 81 illustrates well-worded objectives.

Panel 81

This policy standardizes the rules for claiming reimbursement for travel expenses.

This directive clarifies the practices around the management of corporate information.

These guidelines unify the approaches to facilities management across regions.

This document updates and consolidates the organization's security policies.

Policy Justification

Policy objectives need not explain the drivers behind the desire to standardize the rules or clarify the practices.

Back in Chapter 2 we noted that we can justify our rules in other documents, such as strategy papers, reports, and cover sheets. The explanation for *why* you're doing what you're doing belongs in a companion document, along with other pieces of background information.

Every statement in the draft document has the potential to serve as a stumbling block to approval, should there be objections to the way it's worded. Too often a draft policy is delayed unnecessarily: someone objects to the wording of the justification or the background information and therefore withholds approval, despite being in full agreement with all the policy statements.

You can avoid that problem entirely by taking all the paragraphs justifying or legitimizing what you're doing and putting them in a completely separate document.

Circular Objectives

The kind of policy objective illustrated in panel 82 is common, despite its imprecision.

Panel 82

This policy ensures that the organization's finances are managed responsibly, prudently, and correctly.

The statement is problematic for two reasons.

First, rules don't ensure anything. **People ensure things; rules provide direction.**

You might think that last comment is quibbling, but the wording of the statement reflects a management approach that will prove problematic for the organization. It is indicative of a common assumption that approving the policy solves the problem, freeing management to turn its attention to other matters. The undertone reflects the approach that "If people just obeyed these rules then everything would be fine."

Rules tell us whether the right side or the left side is good or bad. Rules can state, declare, confirm, clarify, and so on, but they can't ensure anything.

Second, and more significantly, the logic is circular. It presupposes that managing finances "responsibly, prudently, and correctly" is an objectively fixed characterization. But the activities prescribed in the statements are to be considered "responsible, prudent, and correct" only *because* they are so prescribed.

The objective in panel 82 would be more accurate were it worded as in panel 83.

Panel 83

> This policy sets out practices that we consider responsible, prudent, and correct for the management of finances in the organization.

Maintaining a Sense of Scale

I have seen too many policy statements with unrealistic or grandiose objectives.

It is insufficient for an objective to be boastful; it requires grounding and demonstrable causation to be credible. An objective that overstates its effect is not helpful to our understanding of what the policy instrument is intended to do.

Some examples of overstatement are shown in panel 84.

Panel 84

> This policy ensures the continued trust and confidence of the public in our organization.

> This directive protects consumers by supporting the company's commitment to customer service and corporate integrity.

> This standard ensures the safety, security, and welfare of our employees.

If I'm not mistaken, the technical term for abstract objectives of this nature is "blah-blah." They may be noble objectives to aim for, but if the organization's management thinks it has achieved these objectives solely by approving the policy, then it clearly has a much more serious problem. In contrast, the more focussed objectives set out in panel 81 can in fact be achieved by approving the policy.

Put the policy into perspective. Most likely it is just one piece of a larger strategy to "ensure the continued trust and confidence of the public" or whatever the overall picture demands. The role of the policy instrument in that case is to set out the policy decisions relevant to the strategy, and the objective of the policy should be to do exactly that.

Statements of the policy objective would be more accurate if worded along the lines of those shown in panel 85.

Panel 85

> This policy aligns organizational practices with respect to …
>
> This directive consolidates the rules around …
>
> This standard establishes the specifications for …
>
> This document rationalizes the differences among …

---

5. Scope Statement

Some policies contain a statement defining the scope of some aspect of the policy — for example, to whom or in what situations it applies.

Scope statements are almost always unnecessary, because

- ✦ the scope of the policy is already limited by the competence of the policy owner, and
- ✦ the scope is just as easily set by a policy statement.

Take the scope statement in panel 86.

Panel 86

This policy is applicable to customers served by the Western Region.

Two possible situations would give rise to wanting to make the above scope statement.

Situation #1: The policy owner's authority is limited to the Western Region.

In this situation the statement is true whether or not it's included, so it can be omitted. No government prefaces a law by specifying that it only applies to the citizens under its authority, and the rules of Monopoly® don't start by indicating that they don't apply to other games.

Situation #2: The policy owner governs many regions and these rules apply only to the Western one.

In this situation, the scope can be set through clear wording in the very first policy statement, as seen in panel 87.

Panel 87

1. The Western Region is subject to the following rules:

Looking at it from a different angle, we can reach the same conclusions. In situation #1, the jurisdiction of the policy owner is a fact. Facts belong in the guidance documents. If you want to reiterate the extent or the limits of the policy owner, the guidance is the place to do that.

In situation #2, the decision to limit the rules to the Western Region is a policy decision. That policy decision belongs with the other policy decisions in the core of the policy, not in the packaging around it.

6. Other Versions

Where the policy instrument is available in a different format, location, or language, then directions to those resources can appear following the policy statements.

It is rare, though, that you will need multiple versions of the policy. It is much more common to have multiple versions of guidance documents.

7. Enquiries

A good policy instrument indicates clearly to whom people can turn when they have questions. A statement like the one in panel 88 closes every policy document.

Panel 88

Enquiries about this document are to be directed to ...

The statement in panel 89 is even more helpful.

Panel 89

Enquiries about this document are handled by …

The sentence is best completed with the name of a position or office rather than an individual, so that the document doesn't need to be amended when the individual moves somewhere else.

Summary

Structured packaging makes policies look uniform and helps you avoid the omission of critical management details. Standardizing the structure prior to any major policy writing or renewal initiative will save time in the long run.

Chapter 12

DRAFTING TIPS

It should go without saying that policies need to be drafted with care. Too often, though, writers borrow language from other documents thinking it's a safe route. It's only a safe route if those other documents were written correctly.

Policy instruments are a special class of business writing and are most effective when the wording is clear, succinct, and respectful. Like other well-written business documents, they are gender-neutral, devoid of ethnic and racial stereotypes, and contain no profanity or derogatory terms.

What follows are some language techniques to help you achieve that.

1. Standard Terminology

You may have been taught that good style in English writing demands that you take advantage of the language's enormous vocabulary. Varying your wording throughout the text would help maintain novelty and interest.

That rule of style does not apply to policy instruments. Policy instruments are not meant to be literature and **the use of synonyms causes confusion.**

Clarity is the prime goal of all your wording choices. Using different words in a policy instrument to describe the same content — even when those words are universally used as synonyms — is as confusing as referring to a friend by different names in the same conversation.

Look at the example in panel 90. It's poorly written, so don't spend a lot of time trying to figure it out.

Panel 90

> Each time a staff member views someone's personnel files, the employee logs the date and the name of the individual.

Apart from the fact that the sentence grammatically contains unclear antecedents, four different terms are used to refer to fewer than four individuals. The last thing you want is to have readers struggling to figure out whether you're talking about one thing, two things, or three things.

Create a Drafter's Lexicon

Standardized terminology is clearest when it is consistent across all instruments.

A good practice is to create an **enterprise-wide lexicon** setting out the concepts you need to standardize, and your preferred terms in that regard. You may end up later reproducing these terms in a glossary to define them for others, but at the drafting stage your sole purpose is to maintain consistency of terminology.

2. Definitions and Interpretation

Many organizations get hung up on this topic. People fight over whether to use dictionary definitions in the policy or to write their own. They argue about how accurate the definitions are and how accurate they should be. They argue about whether the definitions should sit in the policy or somewhere else.

Those arguments take us completely off track. They stop us from focussing on deciding what the right rule is; instead, we end up arguing over what makes a good definition.

To my mind, the culprit is the term "definition." I prefer the term "**interpretation**." So do a number of governments, using the heading "interpretation" in statutes and regulations as a matter of course.

"Interpretation" has a distinct advantage: it reduces the amount of information we need to provide about the term. Supplementing a word's meaning is far easier for most of us than drafting a full definition, and we can leave the writing of real definitions to the dictionaries.

Under an "Interpretation" provision, you might insert statements like those in panel 91.

Panel 91

In this policy,

(a) "current customers" refers to customers who have made a purchase within the past five years

(b) "employees" includes contract workers

(c) "Ericaceae" include Monotropoideae and Styphelioideae but not Cassiopoideae

(d) "main offices" excludes offices in the southeast region, and

(e) "personal information" is to be interpreted according to locally applicable privacy protection laws.

As you can clearly see, these statements do not even pretend to be definitions. What the statements do is help us understand the way the term is used in the document.

If you tripped on sub-paragraph (c) in that last example, you're not alone. I don't understand it, either. But so what? **The purpose of the interpretation statement is not to teach us about the subject; it's to let us know how the drafters wanted to use the term.**

If the purpose of an interpretation statement is to help non-experts understand a term, then that statement belongs in the guidance documents.

Potential for Confusion

You might think you're being helpful by explaining a term for non-experts in the policy statement, but that explanation has the potential to create ambiguities.

Take the phrase "including customs duties" in panel 92.

Panel 92

We reimburse travel expenses, including customs duties, when claims are accompanied by original receipts.

Does this statement mean that

(a) customs duties are considered travel expenses, or

(b) they're considered separate expenses but reimbursed along with the travel expenses?

If (a) is true and customs duties are indeed considered by the experts to be travel expenses, then the correct statement is found in panel 93.

Panel 93

We reimburse travel expenses when accompanied by original receipts.

The experts understand what that includes, and the guidance documents can explain it to the rest of us.

In contrast, if (b) is true, then using one of the statements in panel 94 provides more clarity.

Panel 94

> We reimburse travel expenses and customs duties when claims are accompanied by original receipts.

> We reimburse travel expenses when claims are accompanied by original receipts. "Travel expenses" in this provision includes customs duties.

Definitions beyond Competence

In some cases, the policy owner does not have the competence to set a definition for a given word or concept. A policy statement purporting to set that scope is ineffectual.

I come across this type of overreaching often in university and corporate policies against sexual violence or sexual harassment. It is common to see the policy contain some definition of sexual harassment or violence. Common, but pointless.

We are fortunate in most first world countries to have laws against sexual harassment. Those laws supersede any definition made by your organization, as well meaning as that attempt might be.

"Sexual harassment" is what the statute and your Supreme Court say it is; it's not what your policy says it is. **If your definition differs from the courts', you will lose that contest every time.** The same is true for any concept where you are required to defer to the legal definition — for example, what constitutes breach of copyright, theft, disclosure of private information, and so on.

It might be helpful to include those kinds of definitions in your guidance for everyone's benefit. Putting them inside a policy to have some board approve them is a waste of time.

3. Superfluous Wording

To achieve succinctness, eliminate unnecessary words. Here are a few common culprits.

"All"

The word "all" can usually be eliminated from policy statements since it rarely adds anything to a rule's meaning.

In panels 95 and 96, the B statement doesn't actually tell us anything more than the A statement.

Panel 95

(A) Individuals present identification upon entering the building.

(B) All individuals present identification upon entering the building.

Panel 96

(A) Managers report accidents to the occupational health and safety office within seven days.

(B) Managers report all accidents to the occupational health and safety office within seven days.

As discussed in Chapter 6, the presence of "all" in the above examples suggests either (1) there have been non-compliance issues, or (2) someone is afraid there might be some in the future. Unless your goal is to alert the world to your issues around non-compliance, you can safely drop the word "all" without affecting the meaning of the rule.

Here are other tough-sounding words that rarely add meaning to a rule, except the revelation of past problems:

- absolutely
- always
- at all times
- each
- every
- never
- no exceptions
- strictly

It's easy to test for dispensability. If a statement uses one of those words, omit it to see if the requirement really changes.

Doublets

Panel 97 illustrates the terrible effect of using doublets (also called "word pairs") in policy statements. The first statement sounds terrible and the second is even worse!

Panel 97

Applicants who plan to update, change, or modify their application forms should send or forward the updated information, changes, and modifications no later than March 31st.

Applicants who plan to update, change, and/or modify their application forms should send and/or forward the updated information, changes, and/or modifications no later than March 31st.

Doublets are an historical vestige of the English language. Whether they still belong in legal documents is a question for another forum, but the time has definitely come to retire them from policy instruments.

Look at where doublets came from. Starting in the year 1066, the language of government and formality in England was the dialect of French spoken in Normandy at the time of the Conquest. For centuries, French dominated the speech of the educated class, while the common people continued to speak various Germanic and Norse dialects that had previously spread throughout the land. By the middle ages, a distinct and documented dialect called Legal French was used in English juridical matters, and French terms were standard.

Things changed when English began to gain status. Although French remained the language of the learned class, over time it became socially unacceptable to alienate those who could speak only English.

Lawyers and legal practice change slowly, however, and the old Legal French terms refused to be ousted gracefully by English equivalents. Thus began the custom of pairing words in formal documents, to provide the Anglo (Germanic) term alongside the original French or Latinate word. Scores of these pairings still exist in the language today, such as:

+ (last) will and testament
+ to have and to hold
+ free and clear
+ null and void
+ goods and chattels
+ lewd and lascivious
+ give and bequeath

The terms were equivalent in meaning but were paired in formal situations in deference to both languages.

After a while, the custom spilled over to situations where it wasn't needed; writers started using doublets even when both terms came from the same language origins. Examples of these include:

+ terms and conditions
+ heirs and assigns
+ agree and covenant
+ over and above
+ due and payable

Doublets eventually became the mark of formality and officialdom. Using two terms together was thought to make a formal statement twice as clear. Even today, many writers still believe that doublets make text sound more authoritative.

Newsflash: **they don't.**

In fact, a doublet makes text more difficult to interpret because it's impossible to know when the two terms are meant to represent two different concepts and when they are meant to represent the same concept. Remember our discussion of the problems caused by the unnecessary use of synonyms? It applies here, too.

Are you aiming for clear and succinct? Pick one term to represent a concept and stick with it.

Panel 97 is much more easily understood when it is reworded and stripped of the doublets, as in panel 98.

Panel 98

Applicants can update their application forms by providing new information no later than March 31st.

And and/or Or

We can't leave the issue of word pairs without grieving over the all-too-common use of the meaningless conjunction "and/or."

"And/or" is the poster child for ambiguous writing.

In the past I tried to be more understanding. When I came across that oxymoron, I'd imagine some poor writer starting with "or," then scratching it out and replacing it with "and," then switching back to "or." The writer would then repeat the phrase several times *sotto voce*, alternating between "and" and "or," desperately trying to decide between them, but eventually giving up and scribbling "and/or."

Today I know better than to think it was an accident. Even some good writers — meaning, those whom you'd expect to know better — use "and/or" as if it were some sort of portmanteau.

The rules are really quite simple. "And" means "both (or all) are required," as in panel 99.

Panel 99

The official company colours are red, green, and blue.

"Or" means "only one is required," as in panel 100.

Panel 100

Company vehicles are painted red, green or blue.

If you want to provide alternatives along with the option for combination, then do just that, like the examples in panel 101.

Panel 101

Packages for company products are coloured green, blue, or both.

Packages for company products are coloured red, green, or blue, or any combination of those colours.

Packages for company products are coloured red, green, or blue, alone or in any combination.

Packages for company products are coloured using one or more of the following: red, green, and blue.

In policy writing, clarity means the absence of ambiguity. The recommended examples may use more words, but they are unambiguous.

Ensure

A word used far too often in policies is "ensure." That word is ambiguous at best and meaningless at worst.

You often see it used in the manner shown in panel 102.

Panel 102

Tenants must ensure they pay their rent on the 1st of each month.

Evidence of the ambiguity can be seen when someone attempts to translate the policy statement into another language. In Canada, for example, where official documents are often translated into French, translators struggle to find the word to convey the supposed meaning of "ensure."

In panel 102, what **concrete action** is the word "ensure" adding to the meaning? Is it telling tenants to double-check the payment? To verify that the payment was received? To reassure themselves? To take extra care? It could be any or all of those things — or none of them.

If the goal is to achieve clarity in drafting, the wording in panel 103 is preferable:

Panel 103

Tenants pay their rent on the first of each month.

Let's be practical here. At the end of the day, do you want the tenants to concentrate on paying or on ensuring? If I were the landlord, I would rather receive the rent than the assurance.

Further evidence that the word "ensure" is superfluous in panel 102 is that you can't find someone non-compliant for failing to take that action. We can hold a tenant who doesn't pay the rent to be in breach of policy, but we don't want to penalize a tenant who paid the rent but *failed to ensure that they'd paid it*. Worse, you don't want a tenant who defaulted on the rent claiming they complied with the policy because they "took steps to ensure" it was paid.

Put differently, a statement that rent is due at the end of the month is a policy statement; a statement that tenants ensure they comply with that policy is no more than good advice.

4. Roles and Responsibilities

The words "roles and responsibilities" are often said in the same breath, as if that were one of those doublets I cautioned against earlier. In this case, however, we aren't dealing with a doublet because "roles" and "responsibilities" are not the same thing.

A **role** is a function played by an individual or group in a specific situation. A role is meaningless without responsibilities attached to it; it becomes meaningful once we know what purposes it serves.

For example, a common role in a formal meeting is meeting chair. The role of meeting chair only becomes meaningful once we know the responsibilities it entails. A role can be assigned any number of responsibilities.

A **responsibility** is an action or duty. It can be assigned to a role, but it can also be assigned to a

- ✦ named individual
- ✦ job position, or
- ✦ group.

Statements assigning responsibilities to various entities appear in panel 104.

Panel 104

The Secretary tracks attendance at board meetings. *(assigned to a role)*

Marie Wong tracks attendance at board meetings. *(assigned to an individual)*

The most senior assistant present tracks attendance at board meetings. *(assigned to a job position)*

The Membership Committee tracks attendance at board meetings. *(assigned to a group)*

When Are Roles and Responsibilities Statements Required?

Decisions around roles and responsibilities are policy decisions, and as such belong somewhere in a policy document. But that doesn't mean **every** policy has to include roles and responsibilities statements.

Take the statement in panel 105.

Panel 105

The finance branch is responsible for monitoring expenditures related to this policy.

Whether that statement belongs in your policy is an easy question to answer. Simply fall back on **the fundamental distinction between documents that set rules and documents that restate them.**

If, pursuant to some existing policy instrument, charter, or delegation, the finance branch is *already responsible* for monitoring expenditures, then the statement is superfluous. Leave it out.

On the other hand, if the statement introduces a *brand new* responsibility for the finance branch, then it represents a decision and belongs in the policy.

"Is responsible for"

Like the word "ensure," the phrase "is responsible for" is often misused. Correctly used, the phrase assigns responsibility for an activity to an individual, but that assignment does not mandate the activity itself.

Take the statement in panel 106.

Panel 106

Operators are responsible for quarterly earnings reports.

Taken at face value, that statement means the responsibility for quarterly earnings reports lies with the operators. In other words, it's really shorthand for "Operators are **held responsible** for ..." That much we know for sure. Any additional interpretation we place on this statement is conjecture.

Similar to the ambiguity created by the word "must," this statement could mean any of the following:

- Operators are authorized to produce the reports.
- Operators are required to produce the reports.
- Operators are required to approve the reports.
- Operators are required to contribute to the reports.
- Operators are responsible for verifying the accuracy of the content.
- Operators don't have to do anything for the reports, but if we get in trouble they're the ones we're gonna yell at.

A policy statement tells us how we run our organization. Assigning responsibility for an activity to a role may be an important part of the way we do things, but it is only that: an assignment of responsibility. It might imply other information around how we operate, but it sure doesn't state it unambiguously.

Clarity dictates that the simplest wording is the best. To draft a policy statement indicating the operators actually produce reports, the only thing you need is the statement in panel 107.

Panel 107

Operators produce quarterly earnings reports.

It really is that simple.

Summary

We often comfort others by saying that what we've written isn't carved in stone. That may be true, yet we find ourselves treating certain wordings as if they were sacrosanct.

Let's fix that. Let's identify the fossils in our writing styles, gently remove them from the stone, and put them into museums where they belong. We can then replace them with something more suitable.

POSTSCRIPT

As Carol Ring says in the Foreword to this edition, "Having thick books full of corporate policies is no badge of honour." Usually they're indicative of an over-regulated and micro-managed environment.

Nonetheless, the need for rules will be around for a long time, as will the need to revise them with diligence.

One challenge is finding the right balance between controlling behaviour through rule-making and controlling it through good leadership practices. Organizations built on authoritarian command-and-control structures have proven to be more toxic and less productive environments than those operating within a positive, collaborative corporate culture.

To complicate matters, as millennials continue to comprise a larger share of the workforce, their influence will expand. They do not tolerate being spoken to disrespectfully, and they react in a way their parents never could. Millennial values will stimulate changes to our approaches to employee and customer engagement, and those changes will need to be reflected in our policy instruments.

We've seen how language evolves over time. Wording once considered polite can become quaint and stiff before we realize it. Choosing good wording is even harder when trying to find the right balance between formal and casual language, since those factors vary by industry and geography.

For all these reasons, we need to be open to repeatedly re-examining our policy instruments, validating their contents for currency in substance, idiom, and tone of voice.

This book, too, will become outdated at some point. Should that happen, please take the advice given with a grain of salt, remembering the context of the times when it was written.

We know one thing that won't change: courtesy and respect never go out of style.

CLEAN DESK POLICY (*SAMPLE*)

Approved by: Vice-President, Corporate Affairs
on March 1, 2020
Next review date: March 2024

This policy clarifies the requirements around office tidiness and security.

Interpretation

1. In this policy,

- + "employees" includes contractors and students, and
- + "supervisor" includes the main point of contact for a contractor.

Requirements

2. Employees are entitled to leave work for the day once their work areas conform to Standard #7 (*Clean Desk Standard*).

3. The responsibility for explaining Standard #7 to employees rests with their supervisors.

4. The Director of Security has the authority to grant exemptions to this policy for a period of up to one week.

5. The General Facilities Committee is authorized to amend Standard #7 as it deems appropriate. Amendments take effect 10 business days following their publication.

6. (a) After an employee has left for the day, Security Officers have the authority to collect any documents from the employee's workspace that they find left out in the open.

(b) The Director of Security is authorized to establish a procedure for the retrieval of those documents by the employee entitled to them.

7. This policy is effective immediately.

Enquiries

Enquiries arising out of this policy are handled by the Security Office.

Other Versions

Ce document est disponible en français sous le titre « Politique en matière de rangement du bureau ».

Last modified on February 24, 2017
Intranet/policies/cleandesk.html

CLEAN DESK STANDARD *(SAMPLE)*
STANDARD #7

Approved by: General Facilities Committee
on March 1, 2017
Next review date: March 2025

Interpretation

1. In this standard, "foodstuffs" does not include canned or bottled drinks.

Specifications

2. A work area is considered clean when it meets the following conditions:

- Confidential paper information is stored in cabinets.
- Cabinets and drawers are locked.
- Computers, peripherals, and mobile devices are turned off.
- Foodstuffs are stored in pest-proof containers.
- Floor space is free of boxes and bags.
- Desk lights are turned off.
- The "No one is at this desk" sign is displayed.

Enquiries

This Standard is managed by the Facilities Office.

Last modified on February 24, 2017
Intranet/standards/cleandesk.pdf

OTHER PUBLICATIONS BY THIS AUTHOR

Unlocking the Golden Handcuffs: Leaving the Public Service for Work You Really Love

These Words Go Together, a reference guide to well-formed phrases in contemporary business English, 4th Edition

The Canadian Lawyer's Internet Guide, 4th Edition

Technology in Practice, A guide to managing computers in the law office, 2nd Edition

ABOUT THE AUTHOR

 LEWIS EISEN

Through workshops and speaking engagements, Lewis shows organizations how to take the pain out of policy drafting. He trains individuals how to draft documents to be clearer, more succinct, and more respectful.

Lewis brings a unique set of skills to this discipline. He obtained a law degree from the University of Toronto and practiced law in the same city for a few years.

In 1986 he moved into the area of law office technology management, a field still in its infancy at the time. He worked with a variety of for-profit and not-for-profit organizations, gaining extensive experience in the corporate support function.

He worked for 17 years in the Government of Canada, spending the last several years specializing in developing administrative policies, mostly for the information management support function. He has written several books and dozens of articles for journals and newspapers, and speaks frequently at venues across the United States and Canada.

He is an avid fitness enthusiast, gardener, and pet owner and currently based in Ottawa, Canada.

CPSIA information can be obtained
at www.ICGtesting.com
Printed in the USA
LVHW060830030623
748815LV00031B/704

9 781988 749068